CHINESE WEAPONS

By

E. T. C. WERNER

ROYAL ASIATIC SOCIETY
SHANGHAI

WORKS BY E.T.C. WERNER

Descriptive Sociology—Chinese.

China of the Chinese.

Chinese Ditties.

Myths and Legends of China.

Autumn Leaves (sociological, sinological, philosophical, metaphysical, and autobiographical).

A Dictionary of Chinese Mythology (n the Press).

Chinese Weapons (extra volume of the N. China Branch Royal Asiatic Society Series).

PAMPHLETS

A Journey North and East of Peking.

The Great Wall of China.

An Index to Consular and Marriage Fee Tables.

Herbert Spencer.

The Mischief-working Metric System.

The Chinese Idea of the Second Self.

REVISION

Dyer Ball's Things Chinese (5th edition).

TRANSLATION

Wieger's Histoire des croyances religieuses et des Opinions philosophiques en Chine.

Wieger's La Chine á Travers les Ages.

ROYAL ASIATIC SOCIETY

(North China Branch)

Extra vol.

CHINESE WEAPONS

By

E. T. C. WERNER,

H. B. M. Consul, Foochow (retired), Barrister-at-law
Middle Temple, late member of the Chinese
Government Historiographical Bureau,
Peking, etc.

PUBLISHED BY
THE ROYAL ASIATIC SOCIETY NORTH CHINA BRANCH
SHANGHAI
1932

FOREWORD

To the Council of the North China Branch of the Royal Asiatic Society I express my sincere thanks for having undertaken the publication of this paper on Chinese Weapons, and also to the Rev. Dr. Evan Morgan, the well-known sinologist, for what must have been the by no means pleasant task of seeing it through the Press.

My object in unearthing, classifying, and illustrating this group of facts was merely to contribute some spadework to the accumulating mass of sinological material, yearly rising higher and higher, which, to be complete, must take many years and the wearisome labour of numerous industrious workers.

E. T. C. W.

Peking (Peiping),

November, 1931.

———————

This book may be said truly to be a "Brand plucked from the burning." The Commercial Press had undertaken the work of printing. Just two days before the destruction of the Works by bombs from the Japanese planes, the Company had delivered the complete proofs, letterpress and illustrations, for proofreading. In the conflagration everything else was destroyed. The author had reserved no copy of the work: and it is owing to the happy circumstance of the proofs having been delivered that it is now possible to publish the work. The Commercial Press has our sympathy in its irreparable losses. E.M.

CONTENTS

ILLUSTRATIONS

CHINESE WEAPONS

By E. T. C. Werner

When we read, in the *Kang chien i chih lu* 綱鑑易知錄 or the *T'ung chien kang mu* 通鑑綱目, of the terrible slaughter which occurred in China's civil wars in early times and those carried on sporadically during forty centuries and probably not yet extinct; when we note that a world record was established in 260 B.C. by Pai Ch'i 白起 decapitating in one day 400,000 of Chao's 趙 surrendered soldiers after the siege of Ch'ang-p'ing 長平; when we try to estimate what the population of China might now be but for the millions and millions sacrificed to China's perennial restlessness and the changes in human history thereby entailed; we are naturally led to enquire as to the means employed to achieve these remarkable if extremely gruesome results.

Chinese literature furnishes us with ample information regarding them. Many are mentioned in the Classics, but for knowledge of the majority and for details we must search in other Chinese works.

The word for weapon is *ping* 兵, which originally did not mean a soldier, and it is with the *ping* 兵 of China that we are here concerned. The *Pai shih lei pien* 稗史類編 says *ping* 兵 was the generic name for the *ko* 戈, lance, *chi* 戟, two-pointed spear, *mao* 矛, spear, and *chien* 劍, sword. I exclude foreign weapons brought from abroad, as not being Chinese. As to the *ping* 兵 here considered, it is not possible to say whether they are all Chinese inventions. Where the inventor or the inventing tribe, people or nation can be identified, it will be noted.

The general division of the class is, of course, into Offensive and Defensive, but some, naturally, may be used for both purposes: attack and defence.

As we have no information regarding the beginnings of Chinese civilization, we are also without any accounts of the most primitive methods of fighting and the weapons used therein. It may reasonably be concluded, however, that the Chinese, in their pristine condition, did not differ from other undeveloped peoples in using the articles nearest to hand, such as sticks and stones, to impress their opinions or ideas on those whose opinions or ideas were at variance with their own. Were it permissible to venture a far-fetched conjecture and draw from one of those curious flashlights which philology occasionally throws into dark corners an unwarrantable conclusion, we might point to the fact that the word *p'ao* 砲, now always translated "cannon", if analyzed, shows us "a stone wrapped up",—a meaning in itself quite significant,—that this character is the abbreviated form of the original symbol, which was *p'ao* 礮, and this seems to speak of "a stone coming in collision with a horse." It is true that stones must have come into collision with horses, and even with human beings, before anyone was able to record the fact in writing, but it so happens that the Chinese character in question was first used only after the beginning of the Christian era, and refers to the stones propelled from machines (to be mentioned later on) used in warfare. It is also true that allusion is made in more than one Chinese work to weapons made of stone by Shên Nung 神農 (2838-2698 B.C.), but these, of course, were weapons of a comparatively advanced type, and not to be thought of in the same week with the class of weapons used, for example, by Maoris or Australian aboriginals. We must be content to remain in ignorance on this point (or these points) until the weapons used by the members of the Sinanthropos family and their descendants in China—or at least, until the weapons used by the earliest Chinese—are unearthed.

A further conjecture may safely be made, namely, that, as in the case of stages of early development in other parts of the world, the prehistoric Chinese got their first ideas of weapons largely from nature, imitating the bony armour of the armadillo, for example, in making a garment capable of protecting their bodies against the weapons of their enemies.

INVENTION OF WEAPONS

Weapons having always been in use before the art of writing was invented, they are ascribed, as is usual in cases where origins are untraceable, to the early mythical rulers. The *Pai shih lei pien* 稗史類編 attributes their invention to Yen Ti 炎帝 (2838-2698 B.C.), and the *Kuan Tzŭ* 管子 states that out of the gold found on the *Ko-lu* 葛盧 Hills he made the *chien* 劍, sword, *k'ai* 鎧, *mao* 矛, spear, and *chi* 戟 two pointed spear, and from gold produced at the Yung-hu 雍狐 Hills he made the weapons named after them. In the *Lü shih ch'un ch'iu* 呂氏春秋 it is stated that the five kinds of weapons invented by Ch'ih Yu 蚩尤 were the *ko* 戈, *shu* 殳, *chiu* 酋, *mao* 矛, and *i-mao* 夷矛. In *Pao p'u tzŭ* 抱朴子 we find the passage, "Someone asked: 'What is the best way of preventing war?'" (*lit.* the five weapons.) The Emperor Chêng 鄭 replied: "If, when war is threatened, you recite in prayer the names of the five weapons, war will forthwith be prevented." The sword called *ta fang* 大房 is controlled by the god of the constellation Hsü 虛, the bow called *ch'ü chang* 曲張 by the god of the constellation *Ti* 氐, the arrow called *p'ang huang* 徬徨 by the god of the constellation *Ying huo* 熒惑, the sword called *t'ai shang* 太傷 by the god of the constellation Chüeh 角, the crossbow called *yüan wang* 遠望 by the god of the constellation Chang 張, and the halberd called *ta chiang-chün* 大將軍 by the god of the constellation Ts'an 參. When about to join battle they should be carefully prayed to. The *Shih wu yüan shih* 事物原始 gives the generic name of the five kinds of weapons as *chang* 仗. According to the system of the T'ang 唐 dynasty, this name was applied to weapons used to protect the body. According to the *Cho shih tsao lin* 卓氏藻林 the armoury was under the management of the Yün Fu 韻府 and Lan Ch'i 蘭錡 (offices), where all the weapons were stored. The bestowal of weapons was called *lan* 蘭, and of armour, *chi* 錡. The *Yao chi* 樂記 explains that the process of inverting weapons and wrapping them in tiger-skins was called *chien-t'o* 建櫜. When this had been done it was known throughout the empire that the Emperor [Wu 武] would not again make war (*lit.* use weapons).

MATERIALS USED

The *T'ai po yin ching* 太白陰經 says that Shên Nung 神農 made weapons out of stone, Huang Ti 黃帝 out of jade, and Ch'ih Yu 蚩尤 out of melted gold. The *Yüeh chi* 越記 says that in the time of Yü 禹 weapons were made of brass. The *Pai shih lei pien* 稗史類編 repeats the above statement concerning Ch'ih Yu 蚩尤, who, continues the *T'ai po yin ching* 太白陰經, also made armour by cutting up leather. The *Huang Ti nei chuan* 黃帝內傳 states that Hsüan Nü 玄女 (the Emperor Huang Ti's 黃帝 great great grand-daughter) requested him to make the *chia* 甲, armour, and *chou* 冑, helmet. The *Shih pên* 世本 says: Shao K'ang's 少康 son Yü 輿 made *chia* 甲 armour, and the *Chou li ssŭ chia chu* 周禮司甲註 that, in the earliest (pre-Chou 周) times, armour made from leather was called *chia* 甲, but now (during the Chou 周 period) it is made of metal and called *k'ai* 鎧.

The following passage occurs in *K'ung Jung Jou hsing lun* 孔融肉刑論 (K'ung Jung's Essay on Corporal Punishments): "The ancient sages made the *k'ai* 鎧 armour out of rhinoceros-hide, but now it is made of *P'ên ling* 盆領 iron. (The explanation adds:) *Chia* 甲, armour resembled a substance or creature having scales for self protection, and was called *chieh* 介, *chi* 亞, and *k'ai* 鎧, which were all the names of solid heavy articles. *Shuo wên* 說文: *Pei k'ai* 臂鎧 armour for the arm was called *han* 釬 (*Shuo wên* 說文) The *Kuan Tzŭ Hsiao k'uang p'ien chu* 管子小匡篇註 states: The leather *chia* 鞈, leather under-shirt, was made of thick leather in the middle to afford protection for the soldier's body. The lower part of the *chia* 甲 armour was called *shang* 裳; to store armour was called *lei* 櫑, and cloth for preserving armour was called *kao* 櫜 (bag or sack) (*Ch'u hsüeh chi* 初學記). *Yang Yu-chi* 養由基 placed pieces of armour together and shot at them, piercing seven *cha* 札 of them. *Cha* 札 is a leaf (or plate) of armour; one leaf is one *cha* 札. The statement means that his strength was great enough to overthrow solid or strong things (*Tso chuan* 左傳 and Commentary). "The natives of Ch'u 楚 made armour out of whale-skin and rhinoceros hide (*Sun Ch'ing Tzŭ* 孫卿子). During a long drought the tassels were taken off the armour (*Chou shu* 周書). As will be seen later, among other materials used were paper, copper, lacquer, various other metals, buffalo-hide, whale-skin, deer-skin, silk lined with cloth, red leather covered with metal, iron coated with black varnish, fish-bones, turtle-carapace, etc. Under the Chou 周 dynasty (1122-255 B.C.) a greater variety of weapons corresponded with the chronic state of warfare. The metal of which they were made was of poor quality. After the general disarmament decree at the beginning of the Ch'in 秦 dynasty weapons were surreptitiously made of wood and bamboo. Owing to the effects of climate, weapons "could not be made equally good when the materials were removed and manufactured at a distance from the place of their production" (*Ibid.*). From the Shang 商 time (1766-1401 B.C.) on, bronze was the metal generally used for weapons. In Han 漢 times (from 206 B.C.) the iron age had hardly begun. The bronze age, as far as weapons are concerned, came to an end in the time of the Chin 晉 and Wei 魏 dynasties (A.D. 265-550).

OFFENSIVE WEAPONS

STICKS, CUDGELS, CLUBS AND MACES

It would not be long before it was seen that advantage was gained, in fighting, by using, instead of a plain straight stick, (*chang* 杖) one with a thickened end or crook. This would be the first step in evolution. The cudgel differs only in thickness, weight (iron cudgels are mentioned) and handiness compared with a longer stick. It was used both for striking and for hurling at the enemy. The club shows marked development, the thickened or knobbed end adding extra weight to the argument. The intermediate forms would be those of the Australian digging-stick and of the early Scandinavian wooden hack. These show the incipient bulging or protuberance which later becomes the head of the club or the hook of the spear.

Statements concerning, and pictures of clubs are to be found in Chinese books (*e.g.* those used at the battle of Lang 郎 in 484 B.C.—See *Li chi* 禮記; and the "large iron cudgel" *chua chien* 撾簡 (*Shih wu kan chu* 事物紺珠), but these very simple weapons hardly require either description or illustration. They have some interest, however, in their more evolved forms. The mace, for example (as a survival of the cave-man's method of enforcing his argument, still to be seen—a symbol of indisputable authority—on the table of the debating Lords and Commons, the Royal Society in London, universities, city corporations, the U. S. sergeant-at-arms, etc.), was evidently in frequent use, either as a ceremonial implement or as a warlike weapon, and was of various kinds. Mention of a "half mace" (*chang* 璋), of "round and pointed maces" (*kuei* 圭) and of the "great mace" (*chieh kuei* 介圭) is made in the *Shu ching* 書經, (*Ku ming* 顧命), *Shih ching* 詩經, (*Chüan a* 卷阿, *i* 抑 etc.), though these are there referred to in connection with a ceremonial observance, their warlike origin and character can hardly be doubted, especially since the sharp-pointed one was "expressive of sharp severity against evil." However, as is evident from the *Chou li* 周禮 (*Tien jui* 典瑞) these were rather "obelisk-like" sceptres than maces proper, though the *kung kuei* 躬圭, curved sceptre, shows an incipient change of form. The mace proper, called *ch'ui mao* 鎚矛 is mentioned as "a weapon of the middle ages" (*chung ku* 中古).

BATTLE-AXES

A split or perforated stick or club with a stone or piece of metal fixed in the split or hole, or a plain stick stuck into or through a hole in a perforated stone or piece of metal, forms an axe, and a club to which a stone or piece of metal has been bound, forms an adze. In more advanced types the projecting part is rubbed so as to have a sharp edge, this being especially effective when (after the stone age) the attached portion is of metal. Thus the spear-head passes into the spear-blade, and that into the battle-axe, retaining the ogee-section (s-shape) originally characteristic of the missile weapon. Some axes, however, have apparently evolved from the hatchet.

The combination of the battle-axe with the spear makes the halberd.

The first use of the *fu* 斧, battle-axe, according to the *Shih wu chi yüan* 事物紀原 quoting the *Yü fu chih* 輿服志 quoting the *Huang Ti Chih fu yüeh nei chuan* 黃帝置斧鉞內傳, was when Huang Ti 黃帝 (2698-2598 B.C.) was about to attack Ch'ih Yu 蚩尤. Hsüan Nü 玄女 made a battle-axe of gold, and this was the beginning of the use of the axe as a military weapon. It was engraved with the figure of a male phoenix holding a sword (*tao* 刀) in its mouth. The god of the battle-axe was Wang Chang 王章 (*Lung yü ho t'u* 龍魚河圖). The *I ya* 逸雅 explains that *fu* 斧 means *fu* 甫 and *fu* 甫 means *shih* 始, to begin, because when wood was first cut from trees the axe was used. And *yüeh* 鉞 means *huo* 豁, to open, because by its use a strong enemy could be defeated.

The *Shuo yüan* 說原 states that the *yüeh* 鉞 (or 戉) was a long-handled *fu* 斧 but they were distinguished as "large" and "small", both having wooden handles. The authorities differ as to which was the larger. The *Shuo wên chieh tzǔ* 說文解字 says it was "a large *fu*" 斧. The yellow *yüeh* 鉞 was one ornamented with gold. Another name for the battle-axe was *liu* 劉 (*Shang shu* 尚書).

Chih pi 鏚柲 was the handle of the *fu* 斧 (*Wu hou ching* 五侯鯖). In the earliest types the head or blade was inserted in a hole through the stick or handle; in the later, the latter was thrust through a hole in the former. Later steps were sharpening the blade and also making it partly of wood, *i.e.*, fixing the metal blade in a wooden socket attached to the handle. Improvements were made, too, by making the hole square, so that the blade would not twist or revolve. The *ch'ü* 瞿 was an example of this method. This, usually called a 'great spear', was an axe used in warfare. It is illustrated in picture No. 55, and is attributed to the time of the Shang 商 dynasty (1766-1401 B.C.).

This is confirmed by lines 1 and 2 of the ode *P'o fu* 破斧 of the *Shih ching* 詩經, the *fu* 斧 and *ch'iang* 斨, both axes, differing in the shape of the hole which received the handle; in the former it was oval, in the latter square. The *chin* 斤 axe, frequently mentioned, was of the *fu* 斧 class.

The *Chin shih so* 金石索 mentions three different kinds of axes: the *ch'i* 戚 with a rounded blade fixed to a tube into which the haft is inserted; another with a crescent-shaped blade and a large, heavy shaft; and the *yüeh* 鉞 with a straight blade.

The iron battle-axe *t'ieh fu* 鐵斧, was named *hsüan yüeh* 玄鉞, the gold one being used by the Emperor but only as insignia, the latter by the princes and feudal lords. The *hsüan yüeh* 玄鉞 was made of copper except the blade (*Shang shu* 尚書). Generally, the *hsüan yüeh* 玄鉞 was in use during the *Hsia* 夏 dynasty, the *pai ch'i* 白戚, during the *Shang* 尚 and the *huang yüeh* 黃鉞 during the Chou 周 dynasty; the colour varied, but the form remained the same (*Po ku t'u* 博古圖). The *Ch'in* 秦 changed the iron *yüeh* 鉞 into the *huang* 鎗 (*Ku chin chu* 古今注). The *huang* 鎗 was similar to the *chien* 劍 (see below), but had three blades, and including the handle was three and a-half feet long.

Its sheath was made of tiger or leopard skin. The *Shih ching* 詩經 says that the mailed warriors had battle-axes with wooden handles, the foot-soldiers being usually only armed with javelins and spears. In later times the wooden battle-axe placed on the front of the carriage was called *i huang* 儀鍠 (*K'ai Yüan i li* 開元儀禮). A battle-axe of jade is mentioned in the *K'ung liu t'ieh* 孔六帖 as being bestowed by Wang Chien 王建 of the Wu Tai 五代, Five Dynasties, and in the *Ch'o kêng lu* 輟耕錄 another is referred to made of *shui ts'ang* 水蒼 jade, being two feet long and one foot broad, with very fine ornamentation. It had been handed down from the Yin 殷 dynasty. Another of fine jade from the San Tai 三代 Period used to be exhibited in the Imperial Palace on occasions of public feasting during the Ch'ing 清 dynasty (*Yün yen kuo yen lu* 雲烟過眼錄). The *yüeh* 鉞 was also known as *ch'i fu* 齊斧 and was so called from being an axe bestowed on high functionaries when they went to mourn (*ch'i chieh* 齊戒) at the temples (*Hsi hsi ts'ung yü* 西溪叢語). The *Ch'ing i lu* 清異錄 says the king of Shu 蜀 called the *fu* 斧 by the code name *t'ieh kao mi* 鐵糕糜.

The *ko* 戈, spear (see below) is said in the *Shuo wên* 說文 to be a flat-headed *chi* 戟 (see below). The names and kinds differ, but if this statement is correct, both would seem to fall more into the category of axes, or chopping, than of thrusting weapons. Thus they are wrongly depicted in the *San li t'u* 三禮圖.

SPEARS, LANCES, RAPIERS AND DAGGERS

Originating in the pointed stick, sometimes hardened by being thrust into fire, the spear, artificially pointed, is either used (in the lighter kinds) for throwing, or (in the heavier kinds) for thrusting. Those of intermediate weight are used for either purpose. But a spear thrown at an enemy may be thrown back; consequently it comes in time to be made either so that the head comes off and remains in the wound, or it is made with a hook or barb, thus securing practically the same result.

In some cases a cord is attached to the shaft, thus enabling the latter to be recovered when the head remains in the wound. The distance to which these weapons are hurled is increased by the use of a sling, made of cord, a knotched-stick, or a more elaborate contrivance. The two former were not, so far as I can ascertain, at any time used by the Chinese. The spear-hurler is however, probably the prototype of the bow and arrow (*infra*).

The single-pointed spear was called *ko* 戈 (*cf. supra*). The *ko* 戈 is explained as a flat-headed *chi* 戟 (*p'ing-t'ou chi* 平頭戟), which was a weapon for thrusting and hooking, and is recorded as being a two-pointed spear invented by Ch'ih Yu 蚩尤 (*Êrh i shih lu* 二儀實錄). The god of the *chi* 戟 was Ta Chiang 大將 (*T'ai kung ping fa* 太公兵法). *Ko* 戈 means *kuo* 過, to pass through, because it pierced anything it touched, and anything caught by it could not get off again (*Shih ming* 釋名).

The *ko* 戈, pronged spear, of the Shang 商 dynasty (1766-1401 B.C.) has a second blade placed at right angles to the iron head. Frequent illustrations of it are to be found in the hunting and fighting pictures of the Han 漢 dynasty (A.D. 25-221). Generally of rough make, later these weapons were highly decorated.

In the *Shih* 詩, *Ku ming* 顧命, it is a spear with an upturned blade projecting on one side from the base of the point. See also *Shih* 詩, *Kung liu* 公劉. The *Chou li* 周禮 describes it as a spear with transverse points. It was two inches broad (at the base of the straight point); the part wherein the handle was inserted was increased one-fold (*i.e.* was four inches broad) the transverse-hooked point was three-fold (six inches); and the straight point was four-fold (eight inches). The transverse piece was required to be hooked, and the outsides of it (where attached to the other straight barb) thick.

The Han 漢 *ko* 戈, pronged spear, resembled those of the previous dynasties.

The *ko pi* 戈柲 was six and a-half feet long (*Chou li* 周禮). The side point of the *ko* 戈 was called *chü chieh* 句子 or *hu chieh* 胡子 (*Yü hai* 玉海).

The *chi* 戟 double-pointed spear, or crescent-shaped lance with a point, is given as among the *wu qing* 五兵 invented by Ch'ih Yu 蚩尤 and made of gold (*Pai shih lei pien* 稗史類編). According to the *Chou li* 周禮 it was an inch and a-half broad at the pointed part; the *nei* 內 where the handle was inserted being three, the *hu* 胡, crescent part, four, and the *yüan* 援, straight point, five inches long.

The *Chêng chu* 鄭注 adds that, at the time when it was written, the *chi* 戟 had three points, the *nei* 內 being four and a-half inches long, the *hu* 胡 six, and the *yüan* 援 seven inches long. The *Fêng t'u chi* 風土記 mentions that the *chi* 戟 was thirteen feet long and could combine in one [the use of] all the five weapons. In Ch'u 楚 the *chi* 戟 was called *chieh* 子, the bladeless *chi* 戟 being called in Ch'in 秦 and Chin 晉 *chieh* 釪 or *yen* 鏶; in Wu 吳 and Yang 揚 it was called *ko* 戈. In Tung Ch'i 東齊, Ch'in 秦 and Chin 晉 the large ones were called *man hu* 鏝胡, the curved ones being named *kou chieh* 鈎釪. The three-pointed *man hu* 鏝胡 was called *yen chi* 匽戟 by the natives of Southern Ch'u 楚 and Wan Chêng 宛鄭. In Kuan 關 and to the west the handle was called *pi* 柲 or *shu* 殳

(*Fang yen* 方言). *Kuei* 戣 and *ch'ü* 瞿 are stated in the *Chou shu* 周書 to be kinds of *chi* 戟. In the Ts'ung Fu 崇福 Gate were exhibited ten *chi* 戟 named *chi ming* 雞鳴 (*Chin tung kung chiu shih* 晉東宮舊事). The *chi* 戟 with a pennant (*i* 衣) was called *ch'i* 棨 (*Shuo wên* 說文). Under the Han 漢 system *ch'i chi* 棨戟, pennanted spears, took the place of the *fu yüeh* 斧鉞 (*Han tsa shih* 漢雜事). The former was largely used as insignia at Court and was then called *pi chi* 陛戟, the name being changed for similar spears presented to lower ranks (*Pai shih lei pien* 稗史類編), the Emperor using twenty-four, and the feudal lords twelve (*Ming wu k'ao* 名物考).

The *shu* 殳 was a long spear. It was one *hsin* 尋 (eight feet) four feet long or one and a-half *hsin* 尋 (*i.e.* one *chang* 丈 two feet long) (*K'ao kung chi* 考工記). According to the *Shuo wên* 說文, it was made of wood with a point of metal resembling teeth. The *K'ao kung chi* 考工記 says it was fourteen feet long. It was carried on the war chariot.

The *mao* 矛, lance, whose god was *Tieh ch'iang* 跌踚 (*T'ai kung ping fa* 太公兵法), is included in the *wu ping* 五兵 (*supra*) invented by Ch'ih Yu 蚩尤 (*Lü shih ch'un ch'iu* 呂氏春秋). The *êrh mao* 二矛 mentioned in the *Shih Kuo fêng* 詩國風 as being very sharp, are stated in the Commentary to be the *i mao* 夷矛, twenty-four feet long, and the *ch'iu mao* 酋矛, twenty feet long. Each had two *ying* 英, feather ornaments, or tufts (*ibid.*). *Cf.* the vermilion tassels and the green bands of the two *mao* 矛 in each of the princes' chariots, in *ibid.*

Pi kung 閟宮. The sharp-pointed *mao* 矛 with hooks bending downwards are referred to in *Shu ching* 書經, *Ku ming* 顧命, and the trident *mao* 矛 with gilt edges in *ibid.*, *Hsiao jung* 小戎. The *Shih ching* 詩經 Commentary says *chiu mao* 厹矛 was the *êrh yü mao* 二隅矛 Some had three-edged, some four-edged blades. The handle of the *mao* 矛 resembled the skin-bone of a crane and was called *ho hsi* 鶴膝 (*Fang yen* 方言). The *tz'ŭ ping* 刺兵 was a kind of lance which had the *chüan* 蜎, the latter being explained by *nao* 撓 to scratch (*Pai liu t'ieh* 北六帖). Other names for the *mao* 矛 were *tz'ŭ piao* 刺彪 (*Pei shih* 白史) and *t'ien shih yin* 天矢陰 (*Lung yü ho t'u* 龍魚河圖).

The *hsiao* 猇 or *shuo* 槊 (鎙). An eighteen foot long *mao* 矛 was called *hsiao* 猇, which was a lance used by cavalrymen. *Hsiao* 猇 meant to kill quickly, and was alternately named *chi* 激, the latter being explained as *chieh* 截, to cut off, *sc.* the enemy's *mao* 矛 (*I yüan* 逸原). It was made with a red lacquer surface and black tuft, was sometimes eighteen feet and even twenty-four feet long (*Yü i yü Yen wang shu* 庾翼與 燕王書; *Pai liu t'ieh* 白六帖), with two blades, and one foot three inches wide. According to the *Sung ch'i pi chi* 宋祁筆記 when the

Sung-kung 宋公 Hsüan Hsien 宣獻 compiled a list of weapons he could not discover the origin of the *pao shuo* 檦槊 and none of the Scholars could throw any light on the question, but after ten years of research he found that in Chiang Tso 江左 there was a *shao shuo* 㪉槊 of which the point was as large as a *shao* 㪉; hence the name. It is mentioned as being used by a General Chin Wu 金吾 in the T'ang 唐 dynasty, and as being erected in the imperial court in the Sung 宋. When the Emperor went out, eight *pao shuo* 檦槊 were paraded before the imperial carriage (*Shih wu kan chu* 事物紺珠).

The *ch'iang* 槍, spear, said to have been invented by Huang Ti 黃帝 (2698-2598 B.C.), had a wooden handle and metal point. It was enlarged by [Chu-ko 諸葛] K'ung-ming 孔明 (A.D. 181-234) (*ibid.*). Chu 諸 is also credited with making a spear of *K'u chu* 苦竹 twelve feet long *Hsü shih shih* 續事始). The name *ch'iang* 槍 was applied to *yen* 剡 wood, which was used in slaying robbers (*Yün hui* 韻會). The *Shih wu yüan shih* 事物原始 states that Chu Hui-yao 朱會要 gave the name *hsiao* 猇 to the white-handled *ch'iang* 槍, and that in the T'ang 唐 dynasty the imperial body guard used the *hsiao* 猇; but it then had an iron blade and a silk pennant. It was in use also during the four Ch'i 齊 and Liang 梁 dynasties, but after the Chin 晉 and Sung 宋 it was used as insignia. The *I su chi* 夷俗記 relates that the army used the *kou ch'iang* 鈎鎗, which had a handle five or six feet long, and a blade several inches long, with a hook fixed on it for the purpose of hooking or stabbing. The *fei huo ch'iang* 飛火槍, according to the *Pai pien* 稗編, was made by the Chin 金 to guard *Pien* 汴, Honan province, and in modern times it was used as a defensive weapon on all the frontiers [*sc.* the Empire]. Spears sixteen feet long used by infantrymen and called *chi ying wo* 幾盈握, and others eight feet long and called *ma hsiao* 馬猇, were used in battle in the time of Kao Huang-ti 高皇帝 (206-194 B.C.) (*Ch'ên chi ju chien wên lu* 陳繼儒見聞錄). The *hui* 惠 mentioned in *Shu ching* 書經, *Ku ming* 顧命, is said to have been a three-corned (some books say three-pronged) *mao* 矛, the form of the point above the hooks making it more of a halberd than a spear. The *ch'ü* 瞿, *liu* 劉 and *yüeh* 鉞 are said by Legge to be varieties of *chi* 戟 (*supra*), but, as already shown, they are rightly assigned to the class of axes. The *jui* 銳 has been put by some in the spear class, but the character is said to be rightly *ch'ung* 銃 (銃), a gun.

DAGGERS

When, in fighting with spears, the top part gets broken off, it becomes, and is used as a dagger. It is a shaftless spear-head. When only stone ones could be made, they were necessarily short, being more brittle than metal, but in the bronze age the blades are longer, taper more, and are sharper. Being mounted on more and more substantial hilts, they become deadly two-edged daggers. And the metal dagger, by further lengthening, evolves into the two-edged sword (infra), which of course would not be effective if made of stone. The sabre and rapier are thus shown to be two distinct developments, the former being adapted for cutting, the latter ("throwing back" to the spear) for thrusting. From the latter, also, another development is the bayonet. (In civil life the result is the lancet, or little spear.)

The dagger, pi shou 匕首, was "a short chien 劍" one foot eight inches in length. It was so called because the point resembled a pi 匕, spoon (Yen t'ieh lun 鹽鐵論). It was invented by Chuan Chu 專諸 (sixth century B.C.) (Wu yüan 物原), a native of the Wu 吳 State, who was employed by Kung-tzŭ Kuang 公子光 to assassinate Prince Liao 僚, with a dagger which he secreted in the belly of a fish served up at a banquet; but the T'ung su wên 通俗文 says that it already existed in the time of Yao 堯 and Shun 舜 (2357-2205 B.C.). It was poisoned even in the earliest times (Shih chi 史記). The Tien lun 典論 states that P'ei 丕, Prince of Wei 魏, had three pai pi 百辟 daggers made, the first resembled firm ice and was called ch'ing kang 淸剛, the second shone like the sun and was called yang wên 陽文, and the third had the markings of a dragon and was called lung lin 龍鱗. The Yü ch'u chih 虞初志 relates the story of a yang chio 羊角 dagger, with a blade three inches wide, which could be "hidden in the brain (nao 腦) and be taken out when required for use, without any harm resulting."

SWORDS

The sword, as already noted, is a lengthened dagger, and generally only possible after metals have been brought into use. The Ku shih k'ao 古史考 ascribes the invention of the single-edged sword (tao 刀) to Sui Jên Shih 燧人氏, the second of the San Huang 三皇 mythical Emperors, who, it says, made this weapon by melting gold. The Êrh i shih lu 二儀 實錄 attributes the invention to Huang Ti 黃帝 (2698-2598 B.C.) and that of the huo tao 陌刀 sword of Huo 霍 to Ch'ih Yu 蚩尤. The god of the Tao 刀 was Ts'ang Êrh 滄耳. Tao 刀 is explained by tao 到, to arrive, i.e. to arrive and kill whatever it touched. The blade, like a bee's sting, was called fêng 鋒, the body was called huan 環, being of circular shape, its covering (lit. "house") was hsiao 削, explained by ch'iao 峭, its "nature being stern", and it "was used to wrap round the body of the weapon". The mouth or opening of the "house" was called fêng 琫 i.e.

p'êng 捧, to encircle. The lower part was called *pi* 琕 *i.e. pei* 卑, low or humble. The short sword was named *pai p'i* 拍牌, because it was worn at the side of the thigh, another name being *lu pai* 露拍 meaning to be seen openly. The *p'ei* 佩 sword was worn on the girdle, the *jung* 容 sword was without an edge and was only for ceremonial occasions.

Generally, the *tao* 刀 was distinguished from the *chien* 劍 by having a single edge and being slightly curved. The *chien* 剪 was used when cutting deeply. Ordinary swords were the *fêng* 封 and *chiao* 鉸 (*I ya* 逸雅). From the time of the Chin 晉 and Sung 宋 dynasties the Emperor's sword was a special one with a black sheath adorned with silver and gold flowers (*Sung hui yao* 宋會要). Various kinds of swords were used by various classes and on different occasions. The best material for making the handle was *chi shu* 鷄瀰 wood, the next sheep's horn (*Pai pien* 稗編). Iron and brass were also used (*Tao chien lu* 刀劍錄). In places where the usual materials were unobtainable oyster-shells, sharp stones, etc., were used instead of metal (*Shih lin kuang chi* 事林廣記), The fat of the water-bird *pi ti* 鷿鵜, if applied to the blade, prevented rust. The modern curved sword is derived from that made by Chu-ko Liang's 諸葛亮 skilful sword-maker P'u yüan 蒲元 (*P'u yüan chuan* 蒲元傳). According to the *Êrh i shih lu* 二儀實錄 the military sword used on the battle-field (*chên chih tao* 陣之刀) dates from the time of Ch'ih Yu's 蚩尤 battle with Huang T'i 黃帝 at Cho-lu 涿鹿. The *mo tao* 陌刀 (*supra*) is also credited to Ch'ih Yu 蚩尤. *Chên chang* 陣障, *ch'ang* 長, and *i* 儀 are other swords mentioned at this time. The same work states that after an emperor of the Tung Chin 東晉 dynasty had been murdered by one of his Grand Officers, wooden were substituted for metal swords, but the wooden sword ornamented with gold and silver was for ceremonial use only, and is the *ya* 衙 sword of modern times. The Han 漢 swords were still of simple make, similar to those of the Chou 周.

The antique swords hitherto unearthed during the archæological excavations at An-yang Shih, Honan, are all ritual, not fighting weapons, and are without any special features. For illustrations, see *An-yang fa ch'üeh pao kao, Ti san ch'i,* 安陽發掘報告, 第三期 (*Academia Sinica,* 1931).

Ornamentation consisted largely of engraving the material with figures, *e.g.* of dragons, bears, birds, flowers, the written and seal character, etc. (*Yün yen kuo yen lu* 雲烟過眼錄). Some swords were sharp enough to cut jade (*Wu hou ching* 五侯鯖; *K'ung ts'ung tzŭ* 孔叢子, etc.), while others remained sharp after killing several thousands of cows (*Chuang Tzŭ* 莊子). The length of the weapon, starting from the shortest, which were only slightly longer than the dagger (*infra*), sometimes was as much as four, five, seven, or even ten feet (*Tao chien lu* 刀劍錄; *Tang shu* 唐書). The *tao* 刀, like other weapons, was either male (*hsiung* 雄) or female (*tz'ŭ* 雌) (*Tao chien lu* 刀劍錄; *Tung pin chi* 洞賓記). Honorary names or titles were bestowed on this, as on other weapons (*e.g.* "Insurgent Conquering General"), and supernatural powers, such as shining in the dark, uttering sounds, etc., attributed to some of them (*Pai pien* 稗編; *Shan t'ang ssŭ k'ao* 山堂肆考). Other weapons of this class were the *ch'ih tao* 赤刀, red sword, *ko tao* 割刀, cleaving sword, *ko yü tao* 割玉刀 jade-cleaving sword (*supra*), and *luan tao* 鸞刀, phoenix sword (*Po wu chih* 博物志; *Li ch'i* 禮器; *Shih chou chi* 十洲記).

TWO-EDGED SWORD

Ch'ih Yu 蚩尤 made the two-edged sword (*chien* 劍) from gold found on the Kolu 葛盧 Hills (*Kuan Tzŭ* 管子). The god of the *chien* 劍 was Fei Yang 飛揚 (*Lung yü ho t'u* 龍魚河圖). There were male and female *chien* 劍 as there were *tao* 刀 (*supra*) (*Pao p'u Tzŭ* 抱朴子), and it was also of varied length (up to five and even seven feet), was sometimes possessed of a spirit, and had supernatural qualities ascribed to it, being able to change into a dragon, for example; and was used to get rid of evil spirits, etc. (*op. cit* and *Hsi ching tsa chi* 西京雜記; *Shih i chi* 拾遺記; *Tung kuan Han chi* 東觀漢記). Sacrifices were made to this, as to other weapons, *e.g.* three domestics were slain as sacrificial offerings to a sword obtained by the Emperor [Kao Tsu] 高祖 which had been used by Yin Kao Tsung 殷高宗 when attacking Kuei Fang 鬼方 (*San fu huang t'u* 三輔黃圖).

Chien 劍 is explained as *chien* 檢, to examine, in order to avert impending danger; this weapon having occasionally been concealed in the sleeve during ceremonial observances. The handle was called *t'an* 鐔, by it the weapon was tied to the girdle. The end part of the *chien* 劍 was called *fêng* 鋒, meaning the after part (*I ya* 逸雅). The *Chi yün* 集韻 says the *t'an* 鐔 was the *k'ou* 口, blade (?), of the *chien* 劍; and the *Tzŭ lin* 字林 that the *cho* 璪 was its handle (*pi* 鼻). The *i* 衣, wrapper or cover for the sword, was called *fu yao* 夫橈 or *fu yao mu* 夫橈林 (*Tzŭ lin hai ts'o* 詞林海錯; *Kuang ya* 廣雅). The *chien* 劍 had different names in different districts, as *shih* 室 in Yen chao 燕趙) *kuo* 廓 to the east of [Shan hai 山海] *Kuan* 關, *pi* 鞞 to the west of it (*Fang yen* 方言). The *Kuang ya* 廣雅 gives further names for the weapon (the Chinese attach great significance to the meaning and effect of names): *yen chih* 燕支, *ts'ai yü* 蔡愉, *ch'ien shêng* 千勝, *t'ang hsi* 堂篠, and *mo yang* 墨陽,

The *Wên hsüan chu* 文選注 says *ch'ing p'ing* 青苹 was the name of an ancient sword. Hsün Tzǔ 荀子 mentions eight other ancient two-edged swords: Wei Kung's 威公 *ts'ung* 葱, T'ai Kung's 太公 *ch'üeh* 闕, Wên Wang's 文王 *lu* 錄, Chuang Chün's 莊君 *k'uei* 曶, *Kan chiang* 干將, *mo yeh* 莫邪, *chü ch'üeh* 鉅闕, and *p'i lu* 闢閭. Lieh Tzǔ 列子, too, names some of an unusual kind: *han kuang* 含光, *ch'êng ying* 承影, and *hsiao lien* 宵練, all having magical powers. In the *Wu yüeh ch'un ch'iu* 吳越春秋 five famous two-edged swords are mentioned: *shun kou* 純鈎, *kan lu* 湛盧, *hao ts'ao* 豪曹, *yü ch'ang* 魚腸, and *chü ch'üeh* 鉅闕 (*supra*).

In the *Shih i chi* 拾遺記 we read of the King of Kou Chien 句踐 making eight copper two-edged swords for the temple to K'un Wu 昆吾. The first, *yen jih* 揜日, if pointed at the sun caused it to become dark; the second, *tuan shui* 斷水, could divide water so that it never closed up again; the third, *chuan p'o* 轉魄, if pointed at the moon, caused the hare and striped toad to curl up [so as to be invisible] *i.e.* fade from sight; the fourth, *hsüan chien* 懸翦, caused the death of any birds which flew against it; the fifth, *ching ni* 驚鯢, if thrown into the sea, caused all the fish to retire from fright to the lowest depths; the sixth, *mieh hun* 滅魂, if taken in hand when walking at night, no ghosts or evil spirit would be met; the seventh, *ch'üeh hsieh* 卻邪, caused all monsters to retreat at sight of it; and the eighth, *chên kang* 眞剛, could cut jade or gold as easily as wood or mud. A further set of three *chien* 劍 are mentioned in the *Yüeh chüeh shu* 越絕書, namely, *lung yüan* 龍淵, *t'ai a* 太阿, and *kung shih* 工市. *Chien* 劍 called *fên ching* 分景, *liu huang hui ching* 流黃揮精 are referred to in the *Han Wu Ti nei chuan* 漢武帝內傳, and two called respectively *mao* 毛 and *kuei* 貴 as having been made for Han Hsüan Ti 漢宣帝 (73-48 B.C.) in the fourth year (70 B.C.) of Pen shih 本始, are mentioned in his *Tao chien lu* 刀劍錄.

The *Tung kuan Han chi* 東觀漢記 relates that when General Ch'ên Tsun 陳遵 defeated the Hsiung-nu 匈奴, he was presented with a *po hsi* 駮犀 two-edged sword; also that Chang Ti 章帝 (A.D. 76-89) presented three scholars with swords named *lung ch'üan* 龍泉, *wên* 文, *tuan ch'êng* 鍛成, these names indicating the merits for which they were bestowed on the recipients. *Fei ching* 飛景, *liu ts'ai* 流采, and *hua t'ing* 華鋋, each more than four feet long, are other two-edged swords which took more than a hundred days to make and were ornamented with jade and rhinoceros-hide (*Tien lun* 典論).

Wu Ta-ti 吳大帝 (A.D. 229-52) had six precious *chien* 劍, named *pai hung* 白虹, *tzǔ tien* 紫電, *pi hsieh* 辟邪, *liu hsing* 流星, *ch'ing min* 青冥, and *pai li* 百里 (*Ku chin chu* 古今注). When T'ai Tsung 太宗 (A.D. 976-98) was Prefect of Hsü Chou 徐州, he was presented by the

Emperor Dowager with a sword named *huo chu lu lu* 火珠鹿盧 (*Sung shu* 宋書). Tao Wu 道武 (A.D. 386-409), first Emperor of the Hou Wei 後魏 dynasty, cast two *chien* 劍, named *chên shan* 鎮山 and *ch'ên shui* 沈水 respectively (*Tao chien lu* 刀劍錄).

In the T'ang 唐 dynasty, Li Kuei 李龜, on his birthday, received a *ch'ien chin chien* 千金劍 from Chin Kung Wang 晉公王 (*Chien hsia chuan* 劍俠傳). Other two-edged swords, such as *lung fêng* 龍鳳, *ling pao* 靈寶, are referred to in *Wu Tai shih* 五代史, *Mêng hsi pi t'an* 夢溪筆談, etc.

The blade of the usual type of *chien* 劍 was two and a-half tenths of a foot between the two edges. The two sides of the back were of one-half this dimension. The back decreased in size rapidly toward the two edges of the blade; from the middle, it was divided into two ledges or grooves the width of the blade. The handle, which was twice the length of the blade, was of wood, had the blade to the extent of one-third of its length inserted in it. The head portion was rounded for this purpose.

In the case of large, medium, and short swords, the body of the sword was five, four, and three times the length of the handle, the weight of the sword being, respectively, 3 lbs. 12 oz., 2 lbs. 14 2/3 oz., and 2 lbs. 1 1/3 oz.

The materials out of which *chien* 劍 were made were gold (*supra*), jade (*Han shu chiung pu i chuan* 漢書雋不疑傳), silver, iron, oyster shells (*Chou chien yü fu tsa shih* 周遷輿服雜事; *Tao chien lu* 刀劍錄), brass (*Pao p'u tzǔ* 抱朴子), the handle being sometimes of wood, sometimes of the same material as the body of the sword (*ibid.*). Wooden *chien* 劍 were for ceremonial occasions (*K'ai yüan li i tsuan* 開元禮儀纂).

In the T'ang 唐 dynasty the head of the *chien* 劍 was shorter than before and was worn under the ribs; it was called *yao p'in* 腰品. Like the *tao* 刀, the *chien* 劍 frequently was ornamented with figures engraved on it—of deer, hills, birds, flowers, etc. (*Han shu chiung pu i chuan* 漢書雋不疑傳 etc.). The head of the hilt was made of gold, ivory, or bone partly for decoration, partly to give extra strength.

Scabbards (*ch'iao* 鞘) were of various kinds and made of different materials, often highly ornamented. Those for the chief's swords were adorned with precious stones (*Shih ching* 詩經).

BOWS AND ARROWS

The bow and arrow were already in use in their evolved form in the earliest periods of recorded Chinese history. There are no references to the elastic branch fitted with a dart, so set as to be released by a passing animal or enemy, which is said to be the ancestor of the bow and arrow. The arrow, as already noted, is a miniature of the full-sized javelin. The origin of the art of feathering it is lost in the mists of antiquity.

The *Shu ching* 書經 and *Shih ching* 詩經 make frequent reference to this weapon: *e.g.* "prepare bows and arrows"; "one red bow and a hundred red arrows"; "red bows unbent" (red being the colour of honour in the Chou 周 time); "bows strengthened (or adorned) with bone"; arrows, quivers, bow-cases, etc., of various sorts. The *Chou li* 周禮 gives some useful details:—

The bend of the bow which the Son of Heaven used required, when unstrung, nine parts to complete the circle; the bows which the princes of the empire used required seven parts to complete the circle; the bows of the *ta fu* 大夫 required five parts to complete the circle (*i.e.* were semicircular); and the bows which the *shih* 士 used required, when unstrung, three parts added to form the bow into a complete circle; the longest bows, formed by rule, were used by men of the tallest stature; bows of the middling length by men of middle stature; and the shortest by those of small stature; these were the distinctions made in the bows for archery.

In the formation and make of the bow each individual generally had the temper of his bow made to correspond with his own feelings. The *wei kung* 危弓 bows, which had great elasticity, shot the *an shih* 安矢 arrow, which sped but slowly; and the *an kung* 安弓 bow, which was sluggish in its spring, had a swift arrow: bows of the *chia* 夾 and *sou* 庾 classes were long in the unbent parts, and, when strung, the curve was slight: these were advantageously used in shooting at targets or at flying birds.

Bows which, when unstrung, were but slightly curved, and which, when strung, were much bent, belonged to the *wang kung* 王弓 class, and were used in shooting at targets and marks; those bows which were of equal bend, whether strung or unstrung, were of the *t'ang kung* 唐弓 class, and were used with advantage in shooting deep into a mark or object: the materials chosen for these bows required to be selected at the proper seasons.

In the winter time the wood for the body of the bow was cut out, and in spring the horn was softened for use; in the summer time the sinews for binding it were prepared; and in the autumn the materials were all worked up. Upon examination, the body of the bow was generally required to be of a red or brown colour, and to emit a clear sharp sound when tapped; the colour of the horn was required to be a greenish white, and the ends or points large and broad; and the glue was required to be of the colour of vermilion, and waved or streaked. As regards the attention to be paid to the sinews, they were required, if small, to be clear and long, and, if large, to be firm and elastic. The horn at the extremities of the bow was required to be square, and the part where the bows was grasped, high; the bent horn surface on the inside of the bow should be long, and the outer wooden portion of the bow thin (*Chou li kuan chu* 周禮貫珠).

The materials used had to be obtained at the proper seasons. The *Chou li* 周禮 says: There were seven kinds of wood used for the body of the bow. The horn should be "white, blue, and with large, well-developed tips." The various kinds of glue used in the manufacture were made by boiling the skins of the animals, the stag being an exception, the horn being used in this case. The sinews above-mentioned were to be taken from the animals which, having the required qualities, would impart them to the manufactured article; *e.g.*, an animal with thick-set and glossy sinews strikes briskly: consequently the bow with his sinews would do the same. There should be no knots in the wood, since this causes the binding to get worn out quickly. And so on. (Those who desire to pursue the technicalities of the Chinese bow of antiquity, the attainment of the "nine equalities", etc., should consult the *Chou li* 周禮.)

A modern writer gives the following description: "Unlike the longbow of the English bowmen the Chinese version does not straighten out when unstrung, but goes into an opposite bend, the pointing of the ends is emphasized until the general effect is given, with a slight sinking in the outline at the grip, of a somewhat over-conventionalized weapon of the type affected by the little boy god, when the well-made string is tautened. Outside is a covering, generally of leather, highly decorated with bright colours in some cases, in others sombre hues indicate that they were built for serious business rather than for pleasure. Beneath the leather there is a lamination of bamboo, and that reinforced on the inside of the weapon, with a layer of horn all put together in a manner well adapted for withstanding the great strain placed upon the union of such dissimilar materials. And as abroad the strength of a bow is reckoned in terms of the poundage of pull, so apparently the survivors of an ancient craft catalogue their products in terms of a pull in catties of sixty, one hundred, and one hundred and sixty catty pull." (*North China Daily News.*)

The invention of the bow is ascribed to various persons. The *I hsi tz'ŭ* 易繫辭 says: "Huang Ti 黃帝, Yao 堯 and Shun 舜 made the *hu* 弧, wooden bow, out of curved wood and the *shih* 矢, arrow, out of pointed wood. They subjugated the empire by means of the bow and arrow." Other works state that Pao-hsi Shih 庖羲氏 (Fu Hsi 伏羲) made the bow out of curved wood (*T'ai po yin ching* 太白陰經), that Shao Hao 少昊 first made the *kung* 弓, bow, at the time of the birth of his son Pan 般 (*Shan hai ching* 山海經), that Ch'ing Yang 青陽, fifth son of Huang Ti 黃帝, first made the bow when his son Hui 揮 was born; and that the god of the star Chêng Kuan-hu 正觀弧 first made the bow and arrow and named them *chang* 張 after the god of the star Hu 弧 (*Ku chin hsing tsuan* 古今姓纂). The invention is further attributed to Chui 倕 (*Sun Ch'ing Tzŭ* 孫卿子), to I 羿 (*Mo Tzŭ* 墨子). The *ku ming* 顧命 Testamentary Charge, of the *Shu ching* 書經, refers to Ho's 和 bow and Chui's 倕 *chu shih* 竹矢 bamboo arrows, being in displayed in the Eastern Apartment, K'ung An-kuo's 孔安國 Commentary explaining that Ho 和, was a skilful worker in bows.

The *Lung yü ho t'u* 龍魚河圖 states that the god of the bow was Ch'ü Chang 曲張. According to the *Ch'un ch'iu tso chu ch'i* 春秋佐助期 this god was under the control of T'ui Wang 推亡 (the name of T'ien Kung 天弓).

The Chou li 周禮, which distinguishes five kinds of archery, gives lists of bows used in non-military archery. These do not fall within the present category, though they must be regarded, in part, as accessory to it in that they were employed in training cadets for war as well as for the chase. As, however, the "civil" and "military" weapon is distinguished in the texts, it is as well to observe the same line of demarcation here, referring the reader interested in the "civil" side to the original Chinese texts.

Altogether, "six bows, four cross-bows, and eight descriptions of arrows" are named. "The *wang kung* 王弓 and the *hu kung* 弧弓 bows were used by those who desired to practise shooting at the leather armour. Learners in archery used the *t'ang kung* 唐弓 and the *ta kung* 大弓. These were "more conveniently employed in chariot-encounters, and in field battles."

The remaining two, the *chia kung* 夾弓 and *sou kung* 庾弓, were for shooting at targets, birds and beasts. Bows used in war were, like the hunting bows, adorned with green bands (*Shih ching* 詩經). The bows of the chiefs had ornaments of ivory; others of horn (*ibid.*). A bamboo frame, *pi* 閉, was strapped to the bow when unstrung, to keep it from warping. To preserve the bows they were kept in cases of tiger-skin, or of ordinary leather. Every case contained two bows. The bow-cases and the quivers were made of seal-skin (*Shih ching* 詩經).

In the *Êrh ya* 爾雅 we read: The bow with the bound edge was called *kung* 弓, bow; if without this it was called *mi* 弭. When made of gold (the horn of the bow) was called *ch'ung* 銑 and when made of *ch'ên*

蜃, clamshell, it was called *yao* 珧, mother of pearl. When made of jade it was called *kuei* 圭, sceptre.

The *ch'un hua* 韓畫 was a bow, as also *chüan chüeh* 弮角 and *hu mu* 弧木. *Shâo* 弨 was the back of the bow and *kuan* 彊 the arc.

Chang shih 張弛 was the name of the string of the bow. To draw a bow hastily was called *ch'üeh* 彉. A firm bow was called *pêng* 弸 and the twang of a bow was called *hung* 弘 (*Shuo wên* 說文). When a male child was born, a bow made of mulberry wood and six arrows were used to shoot in all directions (*Nei tsê* 內則). The *hu* 弧 bow was used for hunting (*Han shu Han An-kuo chuan* 漢書韓安國傳). When made of wood, the weapon was called *hu* 弧, when of horn, *kung* 弓 (*Shih ku chu* 師古注). All the archers, when learning to shoot, were given the *chu kung* 竹弓, bamboo bow, and the *chüeh kung* 角弓, horn bow, one being entrusted to each two men (*Chin ling* 晉令). In the time of Sung Ching-kung 宋景公 a bow-maker presented him with a bow which he had taken nine years to make. Three days after his return home the bow-maker suddenly died through having exhausted his strength in making the bow. Later, when Sung Ching-kung 宋景公 ascended the plateau to go to the hunting park, an arrow shot from that bow flew so far that it went beyond the Hsi Pa 西霸 Hill and to the east of P'eng Ch'êng 彭城, and then pierced a large stone.

When the country of Lu 魯 attacked Ch'i 齊 the officers exhibited the Yen Kao 顏高 bow of six *chün* 鈞, thirty catties, strength. All the soldiers competed in examining it carefully (*Tso chuan* 左傳). Yang K'an 羊侃 was born with a strong constitution. He could draw a bow of twenty *tan* 石, and six *tan* 石 on horseback.

The skilful workers, according to the four seasons, used six sorts of materials to make a bow; namely, the trunk, horn, muscle, glue, lacquer, and silk; each with the appropriate quality to withstand the destructive effects of nature. The best trunk was *ch'i chê* 七柘 and *i* 檍; *yen* 檿, *sang* 桑, *chu* 橘, *mu kua* 木瓜 and *ching* 荆 were the next; but the bamboo *chu* 竹, one was inferior. The trunk should be black and red; the horns of the calf were light; of the old cow weak; but those of the lean cow were dark. The light and strong horn was the best of all. The best lacquer was of a red colour, such as *lu chiao* 鹿膠, *ch'ing pai ma chiao* 青白馬膠, *ch'ih pai niu chiao* 赤白牛膠, *huo ch'ih shu chiao* 火赤鼠膠, *hei yü chiao* 黑魚膠 and *êrh hsi chiao* 餌犀膠. When making a bow, in winter they cut the trunk, in spring melted the horns, in summer extracted the gut, and in autumn combined the three materials. To make a bow with strong material and skill adapted to the seasons, was called *san chün* 三鈞 three equalizings. If the horn was inferior to the trunk, and the trunk to the gut, it was called *san chün* 三鈞. If the trunk was superior to the horn, and the horn superior to the gut it was called *chiu ho* 九和. If the horn was examined and found to be excellent, the bow was called *kou kung* 句弓. If the trunk was examined and found to be excellent the bow was called *hou kung* 侯弓. If the muscle was examined and found to be excellent the bow was named *shên kung* 深弓. (*Chou li* 周禮): The horn of Yen 燕 and the trunk of Ching 荆 were the best sort of materials (*ibid.* and *K'ao kung chi* 考工記; *Kuo p'u Mao shih shih i* 郭璞毛詩拾遺). Mao 毛 stated that the bow was adorned with ivory; in the *Tso chuan* 左傳 it is stated that the left hand held the bow, which was adorned with ivory, and now the people of the west country use deer and rhinoceros-horn to make bows (*Kuo p'u Mao shih shih i* 郭璞毛詩拾遺). Chin P'ing Kung 晉平公 sent some workers to make bows. After three years the bows were finished. The trunk grew on the top of T'ai Shan 太山, being heated by the sun and moon three times daily. The bow was adorned with the horn of the Yen 燕 cow, wrapped round with *Ching mi* 荆糜 gut and dyed with *Ho yü* 河魚 varnish. The trunk, horn, gut and lacquer were the best of all materials.

T'ang T'ai Tsung 唐太宗 (A.D. 607-50) speaking to Hsiao Yu 蕭瑀 explained that when a child he had possessed more than ten bows and in conversation with the maker had discovered that if the arch of the bow was not "upright" all the streaks were uneven. Consequently the arrow did not shoot true, however capable the archer. Thus he learned how to judge bows (*T'ung chien pên chi* 通鑑本紀). In the *Hua ts'ui wei chih an yo shih* 華翠微治安藥石, we read: When the bow of Ma Huang 馬蝗, which was made of the horn of the large cow, was drawn in full the string assumed the round shape of a fan, being neither too tight nor too loose. The *Ni ch'iu mien* 泥鰍面 bow was made from young cow's horn. When drawn to the full, the string was as loose as a broken bamboo, neither tight nor loose. This work also explains the method of fixing the gut on the back of the bow. The bow was first dried in the sun for fifteen days; if there was no sunshine, it was exposed for a month. If when the bow had been covered with gut several thickness, the inner gut was damp and the outer very dry, the bow would not last more than three months. The methods of dyeing, lacquering, binding and decorating the bow are also detailed.

As to training in the use of the bow, the *Fêng ch'uang hsiao tu* 楓窗小牘 states that the best archers could draw a bow of nine *tou* 斗, the next one of eight *tou* 斗, and the third class one of seven *tou* 斗. This was the test in the tenth moon of the first year of Hsi Ning 熙甯 (A.D. 1068). In the sixth year (says the Ch'ang Pien 長編), the Emperor issued a mandate fixing the lengths of the various classes of bows, the first being four feet eight and half inches (with an arrow of eight and half inches), and the other two classes shorter by half an inch (with the arrow shorter by an inch). In the first year (A.D. 1403) of Yung Lo 永樂 by imperial mandate the bow was broadened by three fingers (width) and its "strength" was to be "from seventy to forty chin 斤," the bows being divided into four classes. In the ninth year (A.D. 1496) of Hung Chih 弘治 the bows were ordered to be bound with silk and cotton and strengthened with a lacquered surface (Ming hui tien 明會典). The wood of the ch'ing tan 青檀 tree found in Ho-tung 河東 on Tu-t'ou Shan 獨頭山 was specially valued for making bows. The mulberry and elm were also much used, the ends of the bow being ornamented with wild-ox and chamois horn. The Tso mêng lu 昨夢錄 says that in Hsi Hsia 西夏 there were chu niu 竹牛, "bamboo cows," several hundred chin 斤 in weight, with very long yellow and black horns from which excellent bows were made. According to the Yu yang tsa tsu 酉陽雜俎, good bows were made of bamboo shoots four feet long. These shoots during growth were banked with earth leaving the sprout free and were cut in the autumn. The best had ten sections to a foot and were of a yellow colour.

Hsün Tzǔ 荀子 gives the class distinctions as exemplified in this weapon, the Emperor having a red (t'ung 彤) bow, the feudal princes vermilion coloured ones, and the scholar class black ones. When ornamented the kung 弓 was called ti 弨, the name given to the bow of the Emperor Shun 舜 (2255-2205 B.C.). The Chou li 周禮 names similar distinctive bows to be presented on special occasions: the Wang 王 (imperial) and hu 弧 (semicircular) bows were presented to those about to be married; the chia 夾 and sou 庾 bows to hunters; the t'ang 唐 and tai 大 bows to those learning to shoot. Servants and labourers were given arrows to suit the bows used by them. The Fêng su t'ung 風俗通 explains that the wu hao 烏號 bow got its name from the fact that so many birds settled on the branches of the tsa 柘, silkworm oak, or wild mulberry (cudrania trifolia) and sang 桑 mulberry trees, from the wood of which the bows were made, that they were bent right down to the ground. Other works (Tso chuan 左傳 and Commentary, Sun Ch'ing Tzǔ 孫卿子, Shih chi 史記, Kuang chih 廣志, Shu wu i ming wu 庶物異名疏, Huai-nan Tzǔ 淮南子, Yeh chung chi 鄴中記, Tzǔ lin hai ts'o 詞林海錯, and Nan shih 南史) without giving details mention various bows (some evidently being named after persons or places), e.g., fan jo 繁弱, chü shu 鉅黍, tai ch'ü 大屈, lu 盧, lu ch'ên 綠沉, pai chien 白間, fêng chao 馮珧 (the two latter being bows of ancient time), wan chuan 宛轉 (later called mi 弭), tz'ǔ huang 雌黃, tuan 貒 (horned badger; the best bows being made from the horn), *ssŭ tan kung* 四石弓, "four *tan* 石 bows", dyed with black varnish, which could kill two persons at one shot, *shuang ming chu* 霜明朱 bows of four *tan* 石 each, etc. The *Pei shih* 北史 refers to some bows bestowed by the King of Wei 魏 which were bound with *lu ssŭ* 露絲, *lu* 露 silk, others varnished a red and others varnished a black colour. In the T'ang 唐 dynasty the *t'ien ts'ê* 天策 bow was much prized, and during the same dynasty, according to the *T'ang liu tien* 唐六典, the government armoury decreed that the long bow used by infantry was to be made of mulberry wood, that used by cavalry, of horn, the short bow was to be used when shooting short distances, and the *ko kung* 格弓, "pattern bow," adorned with various colours, was to be reserved for ceremonial occasions. A *shên pei* 神臂 supernatural punishment bow, of antique pattern is referred to in the *Shan t'ang ssŭ k'ao* 山堂肆考 as having been seen in use by a country-man and ordered by the General Han 韓 to be copied and used by his troops. When presented to the Emperor it was given the name of *k'o ti* 克敵, "able to oppose" bow. Two still stronger bows than this, named *chin ch'uang tzŭ* 進床子 are mentioned, under the date of the sixth year (A.D. 1083) of Yüan Fêng 元豐 of the Emperor Shên Tsung 神宗 (A.D. 1068-86) (*Ch'ün shu k'ao so* 羣書考索). A *hu* 弧 bow of bamboo is mentioned in the *Nan chou i wu chih* 南州異物志 as being used in the Southern Wu Hu 烏滸 country, and the *Wei chih* 魏志 refers to the *i lou* 挹婁 bow being as strong as the crossbow (*v. infra*), and the *Nan Man chuan* 南蠻傳 describes the skill of the *P'u Tzŭ* 樸子 savages in using their wooden bows and short poisoned arrows.

BOW-STRINGS

The king of Yüeh 越, when preparing to conquer Wu 吳 made bow-strings from the hemp grown on the Ma hsiu 麻休 Hills (*Yüeh chüeh shu* 越絕書). The Li 黎 tribes of Hainan 海南 made bowstrings of rattan for their long wooden bows (*Pai shih lei pien* 稗史類編).

BOWCASES

The invention of these (*kung tai* 弓袋) is attributed to the Emperor Shun 舜 (2255-2205 B.C.) (*Wu yüan* 物原). The names given to this implement were *tu* 韇 *kao* 韟, *t'ao* 弢, *hên chien* 韔韃 (*Ch'i wu tsung lun* 器物總論), and *chin t'ao kang* 錦韜杠 (*Yün fu* 韻府). They were sometimes made of tiger-skin (*Shih Ch'in fêng* 詩秦風).

Kung ch'ing 弓檠, a forma, box or stand for a bow, was called *pi* 柲. When the bow was unstrung, the *kung ch'ing* 弓檠, made of bamboo, was adjusted to it, in order to prevent it being injured (*Chou li chêng chu* 周禮鄭注). The *K'ao kung chi* 考工記 says that bows were put in special frames during winter, and their proper shape was thus preserved.

THUMB-PIECES

Chüeh shih 決拾, thumb-pieces. Chüeh 決 (in modern times called *chi chi* 擠機) explained in the Commentary to *Shih hsiao ya* 詩小雅 as being made of ivory and put on the thumb of the right hand for pulling the string. The *shih* 拾 (also called *sui* 遂) was made of skin or leather and adjusted to the left arm for pulling the string (*Shu wu i ming su* 庶物異名疏). When not in use, the *sui* 遂 was called *shih* 拾 or *lien* 斂. Pieces called *shê* 韘 or *t'a* 沓, made of red reeds, are mentioned in the same work as being rings for the fore, middle, and ring fingers. They were used for pulling the bowstring.

CROSSBOWS

The invention of the *nu* 弩 crossbow is ascribed to Huang Ti 黃帝 (2698-2598 B.C.) (*Ku shih k'ao* 古史考). Its god was Yüan Wang 遠望 (*T'ai kung ping fa* 太公兵法). It was made from a bow *kung* 弓 which threw a bullet (*tan* 彈). It is mentioned in the *Lung yü ho t'u* 龍魚河圖, which states that Ch'ih Yu 蚩尤 made a large *nu* 弩 as well as the *chang* 杖, staff, *tao* 刀, sword, and *chi* 戟, halberd (*Pai shih lei pien* 稗史類編). The name means *nu* 怒, anger. Its handle was called *pi* 臂, arm, its string was called *ya* 牙, teeth, and the outside of the *ya* 牙 was called *kuo* 郭, which protected the *ya* 牙. The lower part was called *hsüan tao* 縣刀, hanging sword, from its shape. The general name was *chi* 機, it being like a machine or like the hub of a door (*I ya* 逸雅), The *Yen fan lu* 演繁露 adds that the *chi* 機 was the *ya* 牙 of the crossbow and served the purpose of checking the string. Crossbows made of stone are mentioned in *Shih chi* 史記. Another name for the *nu* 弩 was *chüan* 参 (*Han shu Ssŭ-ma Ch'ien chuan* 漢書司馬遷傳). The *Yen Shih-ku Han shu chu* 顏師古漢書注 states that when the crossbow of that time was drawn by the hand the act was called *pi chang* 臂張, when by the foot *chüeh chang* 蹶張. The King of Shu 蜀 called it *Pai pu wang* 百步王, hundred paces Prince (*Ch'ing i lu* 清異錄). Some were ornamented with silver and engraved with figures of birds (*Po ku t'u* 博古圖). Crossbows were used to shoot from the war-chariots as well as in guerilla warfare (*Chou li* 周禮). Various other kinds and names for the weapon were *hsi-tzŭ* 谿子, *shao-fu* 少府, *shih-li* 時力, *chü-lai* 距來, (*Pao piao chu* 鮑彪注), *pai-ti* 白的 (*Hua yang kuo chih* 華陽國志), *pa-niu* 八牛,

(used at the beginning of the Han 漢 dynasty against the Ch'u 楚 troops) (Chih Ku tzŭ 氶縠子), *ta-huang* 大黄 (*Shu wu i ming su* 庶物異名疏), *huang chien* 黄肩 and *ts'an lien* 參連 (*Han shu chu* 漢書注), *pi chang* 擘張, *chüeh kung* 角弓, *mu tan* 木單, *ta mu tan* 大木單, *chu kan* 竹竿, *ta chu kan* 大竹竿, *fu yüan* 伏遠 (the last seven being named in the T'ang 唐 armoury instructions), *pien chia* 偏架 (*Pi t'an* 筆談), *chuang tzŭ* 牀子 (*Shan hu kou shih hua* 珊瑚鉤詩話), *chiu niu* 九牛, which shot spears instead of arrows (but this statement of the Chao 晁 history is questioned in the *Wei liao wêng ching wai tsa ch'ao* 魏了翁經 外雜鈔 which also states that the *lien nu* 連弩 of Li Ling 李陵 was similar to the *ho shan* 合蟬 of that time which was made of two crossbows with one string, *huang lien* 黄連, *pai chu* 百竹, *pa tan* 八檐, and *shuang kung* 雙弓. It could penetrate a thick wall from a great distance (*Wu ching tsung yao* 武經總要). The *Chan kuo ts'ê* 戰國策 says that the strongest kinds were made in the country of the Han 韓, and these could shoot to a distance of more than six hundred feet. Used on other occasions it was said to be able to pierce three horses at a distance of three *li* 里. Chu-ko Liang 諸葛亮, of *San Kuo chih* 三國志 fame, is credited with the invention of a crossbow named *yüan jung* 元戎, which shot ten iron arrows simultaneously (*San Kuo chih* 三國志). The *Ch'ing i lu* 清異錄 mentions another in which, by pressing one main catch, twelve arrows were expelled from a corresponding number of small catches and were shot to a great distance. It adds that the people of Chin 晉 feared this crossbow so greatly that they named it *chi chiu chang* 急就章 "rapid immediate pattern". The *tu yuan* 獨轅 crossbow was lighter than the *chiu niu* 九牛 crossbow and much more convenient to carry, it requiring fewer men to bear it (*Ch'ün shu k'ao so* 羣書考索). A *shên pi kung* 神臂弓, made of mulberry wood, the ends of sandalwood, the points of iron, the body of brass, and the string of hemp, was invented by Li Ting 李定, a man of the people, and presented to the Emperor (Shên Tsung 神宗 A.D. 1068-86) in the year A.D. 1068. It could pierce a large elm from a distance of one hundred and forty paces. This so impressed the Emperor that he ordered others to be made, and it is said in the same text that this crossbow is used to the present day (*Ch'ü wei chiu wên* 曲洧舊聞).

The *san kung tou tzŭ* 三弓斗子 crossbow was made by tying two bows together, and required several persons to draw it; it shot several arrows simultaneously, killing ten persons at a time. It was also called *pa niu ma nu* 八牛馬弩.

The Chou li 周禮 gives the bow names *chia* 夾, *sou* 庾, *t'ang* 唐 and *ta* 大 to the crossbows (see *supra*, under *Bows*). Repeating bows (*lien fa nu* 連發弩) are illustrated in *T'ien kung k'ai wu* 天工開物 (see illust. No. 12). They shot from two to ten arrows, a fresh arrow slipping instantaneously into the place of the one discharged.

Under the Han 漢 rulers, about the beginning of the second century A.D., plain, undecorated, bronze triggers, not previously depicted, are found in use. They are shown in three makes: a simple make, with the lever above; another, with the lever below; and a third, in which the lever can be released both above and below.

The principles used in the repeating crossbow were adequate to provide for the rapid discharge of two to ten or more quarrels in succession. Above the bow and its stock, there was a magazine, with a sliding lid. Into this were dropped the projectiles, and by means of a lever the string was stretched into firing position, a quarrel dropped into the breach, and a trigger pulled.

ARROWS

Huang Ti 黃帝, Yao 堯 and Shun 舜 are said, in the *I hsi tz'ŭ* 易繫辭, to have made arrows of sandalwood. The invention is otherwise ascribed to Shao Hao 少昊 (2598-2514 B.C.) (*Shan-hai ching* 山海經), and to Huang Ti's 黃帝 Great Officer Mou I 牟夷 (*Shih pên* 世本). The god of the arrow was Hsü Chang 續長 (*T'ai kung ping fa* 太公兵法). *Shih* 矢 meant "straight," and *chien* 箭 was the name of a bamboo from which arrows were made. When the bamboo had grown to be ten feet high and each section was three feet long, it was cut up to make arrows. A metal point was fixed on the end, and the shaft adorned with feathers. Some bamboos were much valued for this purpose, such as those which grew in the lake of Yün Mêng 雲夢 or of the Fên Hu 妢胡 country (*Kuo p'u fang yen chu* 郭璞方言注; *Ch'i wu tsa shuo* 器物雜說). The *Hsieh shih shih yüan* 謝氏詩源 relates that a man Kêng ying 更嬴, a skilful archer, to convince his doubting wife, let her tie a bag to his arrow, which he then shot into the sky and, literally "bagged" a cloud! Hence the arrow was named *so yün* 鎖雲, lock-up a cloud. The *Ch'ing i lu* 清異錄 mentions that Wang Chien 王建, king of Shu 蜀, gave the name of *fei lang* 飛郎, "flying gentleman", to the arrow as a secret code-word when speaking to his troops.

Other names for the arrow are *ti* 鏑 *i.e. ti* 敵, to defend; *tsu* 鏃, *i.e. tsu* 族, to destroy; *kang* 釭, *i.e. chiao* 銨, because of the blade fastened to the end (*chiao jên* 交刃); the "body" was called *kan* 幹, the support of the weapon; the side was *yü* 羽, wings, being like the wings of a bird; the "handle" was called *kua* 栝; *i.e. hui* 會, to touch or meet, being the place where the string was fastened to it; the side of the *kuo* 栝 was called *ch'a* 叉, from its resemblance to a fork (*I ya* 逸雅).

Other names, such as *hou* 鍭 in Chiang huai 江淮, were given to the arrow in different localities. The three-pronged arrow was called *yang-t'ou* 羊頭. The broad and long one with a fine point was called *chia* 錍 or *pa* 鈀, but the short one with a long point was known as *chia-lu* 錍鑪 (*Fang yen* 方言). The bone arrow was called *pao* 骲, the metal one *ti* 鏑, the one which made a ringing sound *chiao* 骹 (*cf.* the *hsiang chien* 響箭 whirring arrow, mentioned in *Chuang Tzŭ chu* 莊子注), the one resembling a leaf *pi* 鈚. These were all in use in ancient times. The *ping chien* 兵箭 with a long metal point was used to pierce armour, and the *nu chien* 弩箭, crossbow arrow, short with a skin plume, was used when opposing a powerful enemy (*T'ang liu tien* 唐六典). Metal arrows with a feather were called *tsu* 鏃 (the *chia chien* 錍箭 of later times) those made only of bone were called *chih* 志 (the *ku pao* 骨骲 of later times) (*Êrh ya* 爾雅). Vulture and hawk feathers were also used on arrows (*K'ang ts'ang tzŭ* 亢倉子). So minute are the descriptions of all these weapons in Chinese books that even the number and names of the different sorts of arrow-points and feathers, of arrow-shafts, of arrow ends, of the glue, wood, etc., used, and of the standard weight and measures allowed for each, are given in detail (*Chih an yao shih* 治安藥石; *Shih i su* 詩義疏; *Tso chuan* 左傳; *Li shu* 禮書; *Tz'ŭ lin hai ts'o* 詞林海錯; *Li Shan wên hsüan chu* 李善文選注). There were also "male", *hsiung mu* 雄牡, and "female" *pi chang* 闢伏, arrows (*Pi t'an* 筆談). Further, minute details are given as to which arrows should be used on different occasions, such as when defending the city, fighting from a war-chariot, in the chase, on ceremonial occasions, etc. (*Chou li* 周禮 and *K'ao kung chi chu* 考工記注; see also *Shih chi* 史記). The methods of making the various kinds of arrows are detailed in *T'ang liu tien* 唐六典. Newly made fiery darts, *huo chien* 火箭 were offered to the emperor in the third year (A.D. 1000) of Hsien-p'ing 咸平 (A.D. 998-1004) of the Emperor Chên Tsung 眞宗 of the Sung 宋 dynasty. In connection with the subject of poisoned arrows, it is interesting to note the reasoning in a passage in the *Po wu chih* 博物志, which states that dogs shot by these arrows did not die if they immediately ate dung; therefore anyone similarly wounded doing likewise or drinking wine would escape death. In I Chou 夷州, where iron and brass were scarce, arrows were made of stone (*I wu chih* 異物志).

"The Kao jên 蘽人 in the spring presented the plain or rough materials for archery, and in the autumn they presented them completely worked up; they marked their qualities," etc.......and tried the bows and crossbows" (*Chou li* 周禮).

Arrow-shafts from the Fên-hu 妢胡 hordes in Hunan 湖南 and Hupei 湖北 provinces were classed as excellent (*Chou li* 周禮).

The *wang shih* 枉矢 and *chi shih* 絜矢 were used from the ramparts in defending cities, and in chariot-encounters; the *sha shih* 殺矢, *hou shih* 鍭矢, *tsêng shih* 矰矢, *fu shih* 茀矢, *hêng shih* 恆矢 and *pi shih* 庳矢 being reserved for sport and miscellaneous shooting.

The *hou shih* 鍭矢 arrow was divided into three portions, the *sha shih* 殺矢 arrow into three, and the *fu shih* 茀矢 arrow into seven portions or divisions; the *ping shih* 兵矢 and the *t'ien shih* 田矢 arrows were divided into five portions. Those arrows which were of three divisions in length had the last part pared away and tapering. Of those of five divisions, the feathered occupied one division: they were placed in water to ascertain their *yang* 陽 and *yin* 陰 (that is, that one half should float above, and the other half sink below the water) and this (the *yin* 陰 and *yang* 陽 situation) was marked, in order to form the notch for the string, and the notch was marked off in order to put on the feathers. The feathered part was divided by three, in order to determine the length of the barb. Thus, although there might be a high wind, the progress of the arrows through the air would not be impeded. Were it not formed thus, and were the upper part of the arrow light, it would sink on being shot; were the lower end of it light, the arrow would rise in its progress: if the centre of the shaft were light, the motion would be unsteady; and if the middle of it were too heavy, it would then fly abroad. The feathered portion being too full, the arrow would be slow in its progress; while, if too scanty, it would fly too fast and hurriedly. The arrow was drawn through the fingers in order to observe its proper proportions, and that the feathers were correctly placed; it was shaken to ascertain that the feathers were not too many nor too few; and the shaft of the arrow was bent to ascertain that the length of the divisions were correctly adjusted (*Chou li kuan chu* 周禮貫珠).

Some shafts had as many as half a dozen notches, the rear end of the arrow being carved from a single piece of wood in much the shape of a tree with the branches cut off shortly above the junction with the trunk. A regular forest of notches was thus provided, these being for use when horse riding, so that there would be no delay in finding the string, while the marksman kept his eye on the target.

ARROWBUCKETS

The Emperor Shun 舜 made the arrow busket, *chien t'ung* 箭筒, out of deer skin (*Wu yüan* 物原). The same receptacle under other names, such as *fu* 箙 (made of leather), *pu ch'a* 步叉 (carried by men), *lan* 欄 (ditto), *chien* 鞬 (carried on horse back), *hsia fu* 夏服 (which later became the *pu ch'a,* 步叉 *supra*), and *ping* 冰 (see *I ya* 逸雅; *Shuo wên* 說文; *Tzǔ hsü fu* 子虛賦; and *Tso chuan Tu chu* 左傳杜注).

"The arrow-stand is as long as an arrow-shaft, three inches broad, and one and a-half inches deep. The ends are shaped like dragons' heads, and the middle like intertwined snakes. The band between the heads is of light red leather. It is painted red and black" (*I li* 儀禮).

BATTERING-RAMS AND BALLISTAE

The *chuang ch'ê* 撞車, battering-ram, consisted of a huge beam terminating outwardly in a conical head, and slung from a massive framework which moved on low wooden wheels. This machine was less used than the *p'ao ch'ê* 礮車, or slings. Of the latter no less than fifteen varieties are depicted in the *Wu pei chih* 武備志. They were counterparts of the Roman *ballistae* and consisted in a beam working upon an axle supported by a massive wooden framework, and attached at its outer extremity to a rope the farther end of which was fastened by thongs to pegs at some little distance from the machine. Upon this rope a pad of leather was fixed, affording a resting-place for the missile about to be discharged. The inner extremity of the beam was furnished with a number of ropes upon which the working party hauled, giving leverage sufficient to project the stone with great force from the pad on which it rested. Some were mounted on wheels, but other kinds, corresponding to garrison artillery, were simply built up on the walls of cities, whilst others, again, had several beams working simultaneously within a single framework. Forty men were required to work those of the simplest description, with one man as 'captain of the gun' to govern the discharge. It threw a stone weighing two catties a distance of about one hundred yards. The larger *ballistae* were much more powerful, as, for instance, one which discharged missiles from two pads at once, worked by one hundred men, launching stones of twenty-five catties to a distance of one hundred and sixty yards.

The incendiary projectiles eventually launched from these machines bore a strong resemblance to the fireballs, made of tow saturated with oil or resin, that were cast by the Grecian slingers, whilst the mantlets of wood or leather hung over city walls to defend them from the assault of the battering ram, the grappling irons used in harassing stormers, and the huge moveable towers under cover of which a besieging party advanced with impunity to the foot of an enemy's wall, are delineated in Chinese books in precisely the forms that are described by the classical military writers (see *Mayers,* in *op. cit.*).

GUNS, BLUNDERBUSSES, BLOW-TUBES, GUNPOWDER, FIREARMS

"Shun 舜 made the arrow-tube", *chu lu* 軺鹿 (*Wu yüan* 物原). Long large reeds used to blow poisoned plug-darts at human or sub-human prey were later supplanted by iron barrels which used gunpowder as the propelling power. The powder was, however, at first comparatively weak and used mainly for frightening the enemy. Afterwards the match-lock was invented, and this, followed by the wheel-lock, led up to the flint-lock. In the crossbow, the bent bow released by the trigger shoots out the missile; in the firearm the spring and trigger strike the light to ignite the powder which propels the ball or shot. The modern breech-loading gun is a reversion to the method of the savage who put the arrows in at the butt-end of his blow-tube.

"In times of antiquity we read [in the *Chou kuan* 周官] of fire-archery and *wang shih* 枉矢, 'fiery darts',.......but the 'flame-elephant', 'fire-oxen', and conflagrations such as were produced at the battle of Ch'ih Pi 赤壁 were effected by means of straw, sticks, or reeds tied in bundles and steeped in oil or fat, and were not devices in which gunpowder was employed......What were called *p'ao* 礮 were all engines for hurling stones by the aid of machinery" (*Kai yu ts'ung k'ao* 陔餘叢考). The origin of this *p'ao* 礮 is traced in *Fan Li's* 范蠡 *Art of War, Ping fa* 兵法 (500 B.C.) to the 'flying stones', weighing twelve catties, propelled from machines and reaching a distance of four hundred yards.

The *p'ao* 砲 is attributed to *Hsüan Yüan* 軒轅 (2698-2598 B.C.), the blunderbuss *ch'ung* 銃 to Lü Wang 呂望, and the cracker staff or tube *pao chang* 爆杖 to *Wei Ma chün* 魏馬鈞. (Sui Yang Ti 隋煬帝) (A.D. 605-17) used gunpowder in sports (*Wu Yüan* 物原). Guns throwing stones *p'ao* 礮 a distance of three hundred feet used in *Pien* 邊 city were made after a machine invented by Fan I 范蠡 (*Pai pien* 稗編). They were used to shoot at Chu-ko Liang's 諸葛亮 rush-carts (*ch'ung ch'ê* 衝車) at the siege of Hê Chao 郝昭 (*Shih wu yüan shih* 事物原始). Three hundred stone-throwing guns called *kuang yün p'ao* 廣雲礮 and entitled "Generals", *chiang chün* 將軍, were used by Li Mi 李密 in attacking the city T'ien Hsü 田戌 (*T'ang shu* 唐書). A gun made of paper, lime and sulphur, named *p'i li p'ao* 霹靂礮, is stated in *Yang ch'êng chai Hai yu ch'uan fu hsü* 楊誠齋海蝤船賦序 to have fallen from the ship into the water and thus, through the resulting noise and smoke, brought about the utter defeat of the insurgents, who were in the habit of robbing vessels in the northern rivers, in the *shao hsing* 紹興 year (A.D. 1131) of the Sung 宋 Emperor Kao Tsung 高宗 (A.D. 1127-63). An iron gun called *chên t'ien lei* 震天雷 is stated in the *Pai pien* 稗編

to have been placed on the walls of Hsi An 西安. It "resembled the *hê t'o* 合砣" but was no longer in use. It could make a loud noise and damage metal armour. Crockery guns are also mentioned, and they were not so violent as the metal ones.

The fore and aft parts of the *tan shao* 單梢 cannon consisted of four poles fitted above with bolted rods; it had four wheels above, on which the rods and balls were placed, so that it could be raised or lowered when required. The *hsüan fêng* 旋風 cannon was placed on a wheel above the main pole. The *hu tsun* 虎蹲 cannon had its fore and aft poles short. The submarine, *lien t'ien* 連天, cannon was an iron or copper cannon placed in the water and connected by a reed as a conduit-pipe, inside of which the fuse was placed. It was used in naval warfare (*Shih wu kan chu* 事物紺珠).

The blunderbuss *t'ung* 銃. The *Yang I-ch'ing chih fu tsa lu* 楊一清制府雜錄 states that the *ch'iang* 鎗 and *p'ao* 砲 being no longer much feared, the blunderbuss was used instead. The *fo lang chi t'ung* 佛郎機銃 was a bronze tube weighing more than one thousand *chin* 斤, some five hundred, and others one hundred. They fired iron bullets covered with lead of several *chin* 斤 weight. They were made in the reign of *Chia Ch'ing* 嘉慶 (A.D. 1796-1821) (*Shih wu kan chu* 事物紺珠). The *Ch'i hsiu lei kao* 七修類藁 states that in the same reign some Japanese were captured together with their *niao tsui* 鳥嘴, wooden blunderbusses, which were afterwards copied by the Chinese. The names of a large number of different kinds of guns (*t'ung* 銃) are given in the *Shih wu kan chu* 事物紺珠: *chi chiao* 鷄脚 bird's foot, *shih yen* 十眼, ten eye, *chiu* 九, *ssŭ* 四, and *san* 三, *yen* 眼, nine, four, and three eye, *chiu tzŭ* 九子 nine bullet, *chia pa* 夾靶, double target, *ta pa* 大把, large stock, and *ch'ien li* 千里, thousand *li* 里 (*Shih wu kan chu* 事物紺珠).

In the *Hsien p'ing* 咸平 year (A.D. 998) of the Sung 宋, Emperor Chên Tsung 眞宗 (A.D. 998-1023), T'ang Fu 唐福 presented to his Majesty a newly-made *huo ch'iu* 火毬, fire-ball, and *huo ch'iang* 火鎗, rifles (*Ch'ün shu k'ao so* 羣書考索).

The rifles and cannon used against the Tartars were inefficient, except the *ta chiang chün* 大將軍, Great General, *Êrh* 二 and *San* 三 *chiang chün* 將軍, Second and Third General, rifles, which were powerful and destructive (*Yang I-ch'ing Chih fu tsa lu* 楊一清制府雜錄).

As regards the construction and use of rockets, there is no doubt that early in the seventeenth century the Chinese were fully acquainted with the propulsive powers of gunpowder, and the numerous engravings in which weapons of this kind are depicted plainly indicate the progress from a mere arrow, carrying a tube filled with combustibles attached to its stick, to the genuine rocket of modern pyrotechny (*Journal N. C. B. R. A. S.*, N. S. vi. 100-2).

The range of the "invincible bamboo commander", which closely resembled the modern form of rocket, is stated to have been seven hundred to eight hundred *pu* 步 (about one thousand five hundred yards) ; and its effects are alleged as being most terrific and destructive (*ibid.*).

By the beginning of the seventeenth century numerous devices came into vogue, *e.g.* the *ta chiang chün* 大將軍 (unwieldy masses of metal, embedded in heavy trucks), *supra,* etc., or heavy cannon of small calibre and mediocre utility. The *Wu pei chih* 武備志 describes nine kinds of matchlock, beside fourteen other weapons, more or less fantastic, for vomiting fire. One of these consisted in tubes fastened to each extremity of poles arranged in the form of a cross, which the artillerist whirled around him in the centre of a *melée*. Fourteen kinds of explosive vessels are also depicted, in the shape of flasks, globes, grenades, etc. Of rocket arrows, numerous designs are given. Of cannon, some dozen or more varieties are represented. One of these resembled the Western bombard, but its use was confined to the vomiting of offensive and stifling compounds. This weapon was designated "flying-cloud thunderbolt gun" (see below).

The *yün t'i* 雲梯, "cloud ladder", was invented by Kung Shu-pan 公輸般, a native of Lu 魯, for the purpose of attacking the city of Sung 宋. It did not need to be leaned against anything. The *T'ai p'ing yin ching* 太平陰經 calls it *fei t'i* 飛梯, "flying ladder" (*Hsü shih shih* 續事始). The *kou yüan* 鉤援 was the *kou t'i* 鉤梯, hook or scaling-ladder, used for hooking on to city walls (*Mao Shih chu* 毛詩注). The *Shih wu kan chu* 事物紺珠 says it was twenty to thirty feet long, with two wheels at the end, and made of bamboo (see illustrations).

Of the various kinds of chariots, those used on military occasions were the *ko lu* 革路, bound with leather, with five tasselated appendages, and carrying the *ta pai* 大白 flag, made of white silk; the *ch'ang ku* 長轂 long-spoked chariot; *li ku* 笠轂, sunshade carriage, which had no hood, but when occupied by a noble a man standing on a nave held a bamboo umbrella over him to protect him from sun or rain (*Tso chuan chu* 左傳注; *ch'ao ch'ê* 巢車, "nest carriage", with an elevated "crow's nest" *ibid.*). For the various levies of war-chariots imposed on the different territorial sections, see *Chou li* 周禮.

Boats used in warfare were the ordinary fighting junk, the "turret-junk", "bridge-junk", etc. (*Pai pien* 稗編, etc.), and the "flying tiger" with four paddle-wheels (*Chung hsing hsi nien lu* 中興係年錄).

GUNPOWDER

As regards gunpowder, Mayers, after a thorough investigation (*Journal N. C. B. R. A. Society*, N.S. vi. 103) concludes: (1) Gunpowder probably became known to the Chinese—though to a partial extent only, and from foreign sources—about the period 500-600 A.D. (2) Projectiles of an inflammable nature employed in warfare were thrown originally from ballistae, the name of which being identical with that attributed to the modern cannon has led to a misconception with respect to the early use of the latter weapon.   (3) No evidence exists of the use of gunpowder as an agent in warfare until about the middle of the twelfth century; nor was it used, at this period, with any propulsive effect.   (4) The reign of the Emperor Yung Lo 永樂, during the first quarter of the fifteenth century, is probably the period to which a knowledge of the propulsive effects of gunpowder on the part of the Chinese must be assigned.

The *fo lang chi* 佛郎機, an imitation of the Frank of Portuguese gun, had a copper barrel. The larger ones weighed more than 1,000 catties, smaller ones 500 and 100 catties. The shell was of iron inside and lead outside. It weighed several catties. They were made in the reign of Chia Ching 嘉靖 (A.D. 1522-67) (*Shih wu kan chu* 事物紺珠).

Mendoza (*Hist.*, i. 130) states: "Such artillery as the friar [Herrada] and his companions did see at their being there, they say it was of antiquity, and very ill wrought, and was for the most part pieces to shoot stones with, or murderers [?]; but it was given them to understand that in other provinces of the kingdom there be that be very curiously wrought and fair, which may be of such which the Captain Artreda did see; who in a letter....to King Philip....said, the Chinos do use all armour as we do, and the artillery which they have is excellent good.... In every city they have certain houses, where they make their ordance and artillery continually; they do not plant them on castles (for they have not the use of them in all the kingdom), but upon the gates of their cities, which have....thick walls and deep ditches, which they do fill with water out of the next river, at all times when need requireth, which they do account the greatest strength in all the kingdom."

"The iron calthrop *chi li* 蒺藜, fire ball *huo ch'iu* 火毬, three-corned *san lêng* 三稜, six-headed *liu shou* 六首, bombs, had iron points; outside was a mass of powder and to the inside was tied a long cord. When they were fired the sound was like thunder. The fire ball was made of two or three joints of bamboo filled with thirty catties of tiles or cash and mixed with powder in order to make it into a ball; the ends stuck out about an inch; the outside of the ball was smeared with powder. The "iron-bill fire falcon" *t'ieh tsui huo yao* 鐵嘴火鶴, a kind of rocket, had a body made of wood, a bill of iron, and a tail of straw, the inside being filled with powder. The "bamboo fire falcon", *chu huo yao* 竹火鶴, was a falcon-shaped basket made of bamboo with a large body and narrow muzzle; when filled with powder the muzzle was sealed up with paper; the tail was made of grass (*Shih wu kan chu* 事物紺珠).

The *Pai shih lei pien* 稗史類編, quoting the *Shih shih* 事始, says that the *t'ieh chi li* 鐵蒺藜, iron calthrop, and the *t'ieh ling chiao* 鐵菱角, iron water chestnut, and others, were invented by Sui Yang Ti 隋煬帝 (A.D. 605-17) who, when invading Liao Tung 遼東, placed them on the roads or in the streams for the purpose of wounding the men and the horses; but this is incorrect, for their existence in the time of the Three Kingdoms is proved by their having been used by Yang I 楊儀, after Chu-ko Liang's 諸葛亮 death, to impede the progress of Ssŭ-ma I 司馬懿. The same "iron thorns", but called *ch'ü ta* 渠答, were used in the time of the Han 漢 Emperor Wên Ti 文帝 (179-156 B.C.). The Wu Yüan 物原 ascribes their invention to Sun Wu Tzŭ 孫武子 (Chan Kuo 戰國). The *Ch'ing i lu* 清異錄 states that Wang Chien 王建, King of Shu 蜀, gave these weapons the secret, or code, name of *lêng chien* 冷尖. The *kuo chien* 撾簡 mentioned in the *Shih wu kan chu* 事物紺珠 was the *ta t'ieh ch'ih* 大鐵尺, great iron foot. A weapon named *hsien chien* 銑錕 (錕 here having the sound 簡), which caused death when hurled at an enemy's forehead, is mentioned in the *Tz'ŭ lin hai ts'o* 詞林海錯 as being skilfully used by Ch'in Ch'iung 秦瓊.

DEFENSIVE ARMOUR

The statement that wearing the *t'ieh shih* 鐵室, that is the modern iron armour for the whole body, was like living in a metal house (*lit.*, like a house covering *pi* 蔽 the body) is taken from Han Fei Tzŭ 韓非子 (*Liu ch'ing jih cha* 留青日札). In the Jan Ch'iu 燃丘 country there was the Fu Hai 沸海 sea, whose waters were always welling up (*hsiung* 洶湧) as if boiling, and the skin and bones of the fish and turtles were as strong as stone and could be used to make *k'ai* 鎧, armour (*Shih i chi* 拾遺記). When [Hsü] Shang [徐] 商 was a general at Ho Chung 河中 he organized a thousand attacking soldiers and made *k'ai* 鎧 armour for them out of paper. Even strong arrows could not dent it (*T'ang shu, Hsü shang chuan* 唐書徐商傳).

Ma [Sui] 馬 [燧] made three rules governing the length of the *k'ai* 鎧 armour so that, it being in accordance with the uniforms, it was convenient both in attacking and retreating (*T'ang Ma Sui chuan* 唐馬

燧傳). In the *Chia chih* 甲制, regulations regarding armour, we read: Wu Tzǔ 吳子 told Wei Wên Hou 魏文侯 that during the war with Chêng 鄭 leather armour was used, but that in ancient times the *ping ch'ê* 兵車, gun cart was used in fighting, but armour was not made of metal plates. But now armour was made of leather, and intended as a protection against arrows. It being impossible to protect the army and the country adequately with these, from the time of the Hou Han 後漢 dynasty armour was made of metal, but it is not known what the case was in the Ch'ien Han 前漢 (*Yen fan lu* 演繁露).

Before the San Tai 三代, Ch'in 秦 and Han 漢 dynasties the troops mostly wore skin armour, which was said to have been made of rhinoceros-hide, but the histories state that armour was made by smelting metal, though it was apparently not much used. Kuan Tzǔ 管子 said that Ch'ih Yu 蚩尤 made armour and swords from the gold found on the Ko Lu 葛盧 Hills. From this it would seem that armour was made of gold before the time of the San Tai 三代, but that gold armour was very seldom used on the battle field, and that most of it was made of leather (*ibid.*). Armour was of three classes: rhinoceros-hide armour (*hsi chia* 犀甲) of seven kinds, *ssŭ chia* 兕甲 (wild buffalo-hide), six kinds, and *ho chia* 合甲 united armour (which was made by taking the flesh from the hide and fastening the latter together). The first could last for a hundred years, the second for two hundred, and the third for three hundred. In making armour, they first made the pattern and then cut it out of the hide. All parts of the armour had to be of the right measure, and each part had to be covered by a longer one. If the leather was thin, the armour got worn out too quickly (*Chou li* 周禮).

Armour, in the second year (A.D. 963) of Ch'ien Tê 乾德 of the Sung 宋 dynasty, was made with cloth inside and yellow silk outside. Pictures were drawn on the surface. The edges were made of red leather covered with metal. It did not extend below the knee. The upper part, opposite the wearer's face, had two eye-holes (*Yen pei tsa chih* 研北雜志). In the seventh year (A.D. 1374) of Hung Wu 洪武 all the armour was sewed with leather cords instead of thread. In the sixteenth year (A.D. 1383) the Emperor ordered armour to be made with thirty sections for the neck portion, to each suit, two hundred and ninety for the body portion, seventeen for the heart portion, and twenty for the leg portion. All of those were made of leather cured with lime. They wore the black varnished iron sections (*yeh* 葉) used by the Chekiang 浙江 coast district guards and those of Kuangtung 廣東. The remainder were made like the Ming 明 armour. In the twenty-sixth year (A.D. 1393) orders were issued for the manufacture of willow-leaf armour (*liu yeh chia* 柳葉甲).

In the ninth year (A.D. 1496) of Hung Chih 弘治 it was ordered that the surface of the armour should be covered with white cloth and fastened together with metal spikes and sealing-wax. For iron armour, forty chin 斤 eight ounces (liang 兩) were used for each suit; for making the armour, twenty-four to twenty-five chin 斤 weight was required. In the sixteenth year (A.D. 1503) the guards in the South were ordered to change their iron armour for that made from buffalo-hide, sewing it together with thread. In the twenty second year (A.D. 1543) of Chia Ch'ing 嘉慶 the helmet (k'uei chia 盔甲) factory was ordered to change the rules relating to armour. The deer-skin girdle was replaced by the t'ou chia 透甲, and the leather girdle by the collar and lower part (chin pai 襟擺) fastened with pewter nails, thus making an overcoat with round collar (Ming hui tien 明會典).

  All the savage tribes in the Ta li 大理 country were skilled in making armour and helmets. They used elephant skin to make it; the head and back were each made of one large piece like a turtle's shell, as strong and thick as iron, etc. They sewed small pieces of skin together for the sleeves and neck. The shape resembled the iron armour worn by the Chinese. The colour was red all over. The head and body pieces inside and outside had a red ground and a surface of yellow and black lacquer. They were ornamented with all kinds of figures of flowers, insects and birds (Pai shih lei pien 稗史類編).

  The Emperor Wu 武 defeated Shang by using the armour made by Ch'üeh Kung 闕鞏 (Tso chuan 左傳). During the third year (A.D. 267) of (Chin 晉) Hsiang Kung 襄公 Marshal Ch'u Tzǔ-chung 楚子重 subjected Wu 吳. When he arrived at Hêng Shan 衡山 he commanded his general Têng Liao 鄧廖 to make three hundred suits of variegated armour for the purpose of attacking Wu 吳 (Tso chuan 左傳). Tu Yü's 杜預 commentary adds: "tsu chia 組甲 means lacquered armour with ornamental designs." Legge's translation (Tso chuan 左傳 p. 419) of tsu chia 組甲 is "wearing buff-coats lacquered as if made of strings." Wang Liao 王僚 wore three suits of tang-i 棠夷 armour (Wu yüeh ch'un ch'iu 吳越春秋). Fu Ch'ai 夫差, Emperor of Wu 吳, had three thousand soldiers clothed in armour made of the hide of the water buffalo (Kuo yü 國語). Hsün Tzǔ 荀子 said that the natives of Ch'u 楚 made their armour out of whale-skin and rhinoceros-hide and it was as strong as metal or stone. The whale-skin was coated with sand, the sharp points of which could scratch and so were suitable for making armour. The armour made out of whale-skin was as strong as that made of rhinoceros-hide. It was called water-rhinoceros because the whale lived in the water (Yen fan lu 演繁露). The Fa shu 發屬 kingdom had an army clothed in black armour (Han shu Ho ch'ü ping chuan 漢書霍去病傳).

The Imperial Guard wore the pipe-sleeve (*t'ung hsiu* 筒袖) armour and metal helmet of Chu-ko Liang 諸葛亮 (*Nan shih* 南史). "The late Emperor gave me (his Minister) one suit each of the armour of Li Kuang 里光 and Ming Kuang 明光 as well as one suit (*ling* 領) each of *liang tang* 兩當, *huan so* 環鎖, and *ma* 馬 armour." "There is no war in our country, and so all armour is useless; please give me all these," said Ts'ao Chih 曹植 (*Ts'ao Chih piao* 曹植表). So Tzŭ's 子 armour had five rings which slipped over each other. As soon as an arrow struck one of the rings the others would close together, thus preventing the arrow from injuring the wearer. The *Ts'ao Chih piao* 曹植表 (*supra*) says that the *huan so* 環鎖 armour was this *so tzŭ* 鎖子 armour (*Chêng tzŭ t'ung* 正字通).

The rhinoceros-hide armour was of seven folds or links, one over another; the wild-buffalo's hide armour was of six folds or links; and the armour, made of two hides together was of five folds or links. The rhinoceros-hide armour would endure one hundred years; the wild-buffalo-hide armour two hundred years; and the armour of double hide three hundred years. Whenever armour had to be made, it was first necessary to make a pattern according to the figure of the individual, and then adjust the hide to the pattern; the upper part of it was weighed, as also was the lower; the stitches were well looked to, and were required to be fine and close. The lining, upon examination, was required to be laid evenly on, and the joinings or seams were required to be straight. On rolling it up it was requisite that it should fold closely, and, when held up or shaken, that it should stand well out. When put on it was desirable that the folds or links should be without irregularities *i.e.*, not like overlapping teeth, which would be unsightly (*Chou li kuan chu* 周禮貫珠).

In the second year (A.D. 261) of Ching Yüan 景元 of the Wei 魏 Emperor Yüan Ti 元帝 (A.D. 261-4), the Su Shên 肅愼 kingdom offered twenty suits of *p'i ku t'ieh tsa* 皮骨鐵雜 armour (*Wei chih* 魏志). Têng Pai-ch'uan 鄧百川 once offered a suit of rhinoceros-hide armour named *liang tang* 兩當 (*supra*); although he could not wear it, it was kept as a curiosity. *Chin Yü-i yü Mu Jung-huang shu* 晉庾翼與慕容皝書 (Chin yü-i's writings to Mu Jung-huang 慕容皝). The path being filled into load-stone, the bandits wearing metal armour could not advance easily, but the soldiers from Ma Lung 馬隆, who were dressed in rhinoceros-hide armour, passed along without any trouble (*Chin shu* 晉書). Fu Chien 符堅 commanded Lung Mao 龍邈 to make fine gold and silver armour with girdles of gold (*Ch'ê p'in ch'in shu* 車頻秦書). Shih Chi-lung 石季龍 was guarded on the right and left by 10,000 soldiers wearing fine five-coloured armour, which shone so brightly as to dazzle the eyes (*Lu yü yeh chung chi* 陸翽鄴中記). When Ju-ju-a-na-huan 蠕蠕阿那環 entered his kingdom (ascended the throne) he was presented with a suit of fine *ming-kuang* 明光 man-and-horse armour, and six suits of iron man-and-horse armour (*Pei shih* 北史). Chang Yüan 張淵 was given by the Emperor Wên 文 (A.D. 589-605), for his ability in defeating the bandits, some *lu-shên* 綠沉 (green heavy) armour (*Sui shu* 隋書). In the time of Kao Tsung 高宗 (A.D. 618-27) Chi 濟 offered *chin hsiu k'ai* 金繡鎧, golden armour, and the armour-bearing ministers wore it when accompanying the sovereign. When he went to meet Li Chi 李勣 (the T'ang 唐 general) the armour shone so brightly that it could be compared to dazzling sunlight (*T'ang shu* 唐書).

The K'ang chü 康居 country in Hsi Yü 西域, at the beginning of the K'ai-yüan 開元 period (A.D. 713-42) offered *so tzŭ* 鎖子 armour as tribute to the Emperor (*ibid.*). The armoury issued the repulations for the various kinds of armour, which were thirteen in number, namely: 1. *Ming kuang* 明光; 2. *Kuang yao* 光要; 3. *Hsi lin* 細鱗; 4. *Shan wên* 山文; 5. *Wu chui* 烏鎚; 6. *Pai pu* 白布; 7. *Tsao chüan* 皂絹; 8. *Pu Pei* 布背; 9. *Pu ping* 步兵; 10. *P'i chia* 皮甲; 11. *Mu chia* 木甲; 12. *So tzŭ chia* 鎖子甲; 13 *Ma chia* 馬甲; Nos. 1, 2, 3, 4, 5, and 12 were all metal (iron) armour; the *P'i chia* 皮甲 was made of *hsi* 犀 rhinoceros, and *ssŭ* 兕 another kind of rhinoceros, or wild buffalo-hide; and the remainder were named from the materials of which they were made (*T'ang liu tien* 唐六典). Yang Hsing-mi 楊行密 had five thousand keen (銳 *jui*) officers who all wore black girdles and black armour and were called *Hei yün tu* 黑雲都 (*Liu t'ieh* 六帖). Ko Ts'ung-chou 葛從周 had a suit of *shui jung* 水瑩 (also *ying* 螢 "firefly") clear as water, iron (or metal) armour, which shone like a mirror, though it was not wiped for ten years. If it was dim during an attack on the enemy, it was regarded as an ill omen. As soon as the danger was over, it shone brightly again. Ts'ung Chou 從周 finding that this really was the case, regarded it as a spirit, and accordingly worshipped it with wine and incense every evening in his bed-chamber, and gave it the name of General of Chin Chih 金翅, General Gold Wings (*Ch'ing i lu* 清異錄). The Emperor of Shu 蜀 Wang-chien 王建 (died A.D. 918) among his officers used the secret name of *ch'ien chin shih* 千斤使, 1000-catty messenger, when referring to armour (*ibid.*). According to the regulations, *tsao chia* 罩甲 was slightly longer than *chia* 甲 armour, and slightly shorter than the throw-on cloak (*p'i ao* 披襖) (*Chieh an man pi* 戒菴漫筆). In the reign-period Chêng Tê (A.D. 1506) 正德 of the Emperor Wu Tsung 武宗 (A.D. 1506-22) it was mostly worn by the *chin shih* 近士.

Horse-armour was called *ch'ien* 俴; its plates were of metal (*Mao shih Chih nan t'u* 毛詩指南圖). The rear part was called *ta hou* 搭後; the neck part *chi hsiang* 雞項; and the breast part *t'ang hsiung* 盪胸 (*Shih wu kan chu* 事物紺珠).

The *Wu yüan* 物原 states that the Emperor Hsüan Yüan 軒轅 invented the *chou* 胄, helmet. The *Shuo wên* 說文 explains: The *shou k'ai* 首鎧, metal head protector, was called *tou mou* 兜鍪 and was a *chou* 胄, helmet. Armour plate for the neck, *ching k'ai* 頸鎧, was called *ya tuan* 錏鍛. In the chronicle of Han Yen-shou 韓延壽 in the *Han Shu* 漢書 it says: He donned the *ti* 鞮 armour, and the commentary of Shih Ku adds: The *ti* 鞮 was the same as the *tou mou* 兜鍪. The chronicle of Ni Hêng 禰衡 says: He [Ni Hêng 禰衡] wore the *ts'ên mou* 岑牟, which the Commentary explains was a kind of armour worn by the keeper of the drums and trumpets. According to the *Ch'ê fan ch'in shu* 車煩秦書: Fu T'êng 符登, Fu Chien's 符堅 grandson, on his grandfather's death, made himself king and engraved the character *ssǔ* 死, death, on his *tou mou* 兜鍪 helmets, to show his officers that if they determined to fight to the death they could not but be victorious over all their opponents. The *Kuang chih* 廣志 states: Ch'üan Jung 犬戎 made his *tou mou* 兜鍪, helmet of red lacquered leather. The *Hou chou shu* 後周書 relates that the T'u Chüeh's 突厥 (Durko-Hsiung-nu tribe) ancestor who submitted to the king of Ju-ju 茹茹 had lived at the foot (or under the shelter of) Chin Shan 金山, and served Ju-ju 茹茹 as a blacksmith. The hill resembling a helmet of the *tou mou* 兜鍪 pattern, the natives named the *t'u chüeh* 突厥 after this hill. According to the *Ming hui tien* 明會典, in the forty-third year of Chia Ching 嘉靖 [A.D. 1564] he (the Emperor Shih Tsung 世宗) authorized the increase in the metal helmets of all the guards of the pendant beads from six to eight. The princes and regular warriors wore helmets. Those of the princes of the blood were adorned with shells strung on red cords (*Shih ching* 詩經).

Turbans, *mo ê* 抹額 The *Êrh i shih lu* 二儀實錄 states that on the night when the Emperor Yü 禹 married at T'u Shan 塗山, in the midst of a thunder-storm, a thousand soldiers (*tsu* 卒) were wearing the *chia* 甲, cuirass. Those who had no armour wound red lustring (*hung chüan* 紅絹) turbans round their heads.

It was said that the God of the Sea came to call on the Emperor Yü 禹, and Shih Huang 始皇 wandered, or walked on the sea. At the court held by the Gods they all wore dark red (*fei* 緋) turbans (*lit.*, wound round their heads red shirts) and wide trousers, and were protected by a large number of troops.

SHIELDS

The shield, in its early form, was not a broad screen like those in use later. It was a mere parrying-stick. This is still found amongst the most primitive tribes (who, in case of sudden attack, would take up a stick in self-defence), only four inches across in the middle where it is grasped, and used to ward off darts. From it developed both broader shields of various kinds, and the target. The Chinese character for shield, *tun* 盾, supports this view, showing as it does that it was used to protect the eyes. A shield made of twigs is mentioned in *Hsüan yen Ch'un ch'iu* 玄晏春秋.

When I 羿 was fighting with Tsuan Ch'ih 鑿齒 on the field of Hua Ch'ou 華疇, he defended himself against his enemy's arrows with a *tun* 楯 (or 盾), shield, or buckler (*Shan hai ching* 山海經). Another name for it was *kan* 干 (*Ch'un ch'iu Yüan ming pao* 春秋原命苞; *Sung chung chu* 宋衷注). The *kan* 干 was made by P'ao Hsi 庖犧 (2953-2938 B.C.) (*Shih i chi* 拾遺記). *Tun* 盾 meant to protect. To the east of Kuan 關 it was called by that name, or was called *kan* 干, but the former name alone was used to the west (*Fang yen* 方言). It was generally used as a defence against arrows, or was knelt behind as a protection against blades. The large flat kind was called *wu k'uei* 吳魁; it originated in Wu 吳, where it was used by the army chiefs. The larger kind was called *hsü tun* 須盾, and originated in Shu 蜀, getting its name from a man named Hsü 須. It was also called *ch'iang* 羌, being made by the natives of that place. The broad ones were named *hsien lu* 陷虜, as being able to attack and defeat the enemy. Later this kind was called *lu chien* 露見. The long and narrow one was named *pu tun* 步盾, as it was used by infantry. The short and narrow one was called *chieh tun* 子盾, being used on chariots, *chieh* 子 meaning small. Those made of *fêng pien* 縫編 boards were called *mu lo* 木絡; those made of rhinoceros-hide were called *hsi tun* 犀盾; of wood, *mu tun* 木盾, the names being taken from the respective uses for which they were intended (*Shih ming* 釋名). The *hsi chü* 犀渠 is mentioned in T'ang shu 唐書 as a shield (*tun* 盾) preserved at a house in Wu 吳. Shields were occasionally made of grass or of bamboo (*Shih shuo* 世說; *Hsüan yen ch'un ch'iu* 玄晏春秋). They, in this or other material, were lacquered red or black, and sometimes were so light that they could "float in blood or water" (*Pei shih* 北史). In the *I ya* 逸雅 *p'êng p'ai* 彭排 is explained by *p'êng* 彭 meaning *p'ang* 傍, side, it being placed on the side for purposes of defence. This was the later name for the *fa* 伐 and *kan* 干 mentioned in the *Shu wu i ming su* 庶物異名疏. The *pei kuei* 背鼠 was a round shield made of leather and covered with red lacquer, which "shone like the sun" (*Chang shih Kao chien chui pi* 章氏稿簡贅筆). When T'ai Tsung 太宗 (A.D. 976-

98) of the Sung 宋 dynasty heard that the Southerners were using the *piao ch'iang* 標鎗 and *p'ang p'ai* 傍牌 as military weapons, he ordered his own troops to be trained in their use (*Sung ch'ao hui yao* 宋朝會要). The infantry used a cow-hide shield about eight feet long, the cavalry a circular red-lacquered one. Later on, the army used a *piao p'ai* 標牌 adopted from the Man 蠻 aboriginals in Shên Tsung's 神宗 time (A.D. 1068-86). Having, in the year Hsi-ning 熙寧 (A.D. 1068) attacked the Chiao Chih 交趾 country and discovered the way of making these weapons, they were used by the Chinese soldiers from that time on (*Êrh i shih lu* 二儀實錄). The *li p'ai* 立牌 was made of bamboo or of wood, and was about five feet long and three feet broad. It was used as a protection against arrows or stones shot or hurled from city walls (*Shih wu kan chu* 事物紺珠).

Shields were decorated with designs of dragons, etc., and these, again, took their names from the designs engraved on them (*Tsao lin* 藻林). A *po* 撥 was a large shield (*K'ung Tzŭ shih chia* (chu) 孔子世家 (注). Elaborate shields were made of white jade embossed with gold and richly ornamented (*Yüeh chi* 越記).

The *lang ya pai* 狼牙拍, made of elm, had nails fixed to it on the top and blades on the four sides. Ropes were tied to rings on the front and back. It was suspended from city walls in order to strike an enemy attempting to scale them (*Kan chu* 紺珠). The *lang chien* 狼筅 was made of the large feathery bamboo, several branches being tied together until it was two feet broad and sixteen feet long. It was said to be most efficient as a protection against swords and spears, and was named "the fence of the army." However, on windy or rainy days it became too cumbersome or heavy (*Ch'i chi Kuang Wu i p'ien* 戚繼光武藝篇).

A curious and ingenious contrivance, described in the *Chin t'ang shih êrh ch'ou* 金湯十二籌, consisted of a huge jar filled with the white of geese's, ducks', etc., eggs mixed with oil of the dryandra tree. This, thrown on to the deck of an attacking war-vessel, not only made the deck slippery, but enabled the attackers, by shooting fire-arrows on to it, to ignite the vessel. Possibly, this was the prototype of the "stink-pots" said to have been used by the Chinese against the foreign war-vessels at the beginning of their international intercourse (See also *N. C. B. R. A. S.*, n. s. vi. *quoted supra*).

The Chinese, like other races, in addition to the employment of material means of conquering their enemies, have also adopted that of working on their feelings. This has a potent effect with superstitious peoples. Thus, for example, they have displayed banners of various designs with the object of their acting as charms and affecting the minds of their foes, so as to discourage them and make them believe that super-natural adverse influences were at work against them. (Some examples of these are illustrations Nos. 51 and 52.)

"The gagged infantry advanced" (*Chou li* 周禮). The gag was a short stick, resembling a chopstick, placed in the mouth, both ends being tied with cords round the back of the neck, in order to prevent the soldiers from speaking and thus betraying their movements to the enemy.

The above outline sketch (which might be extended and elaborated almost indefinitely) of a vast subject will serve to give some idea of the weapons by means of which the Chinese were enabled to achieve the remarkable results referred to at the beginning of this paper. I have not described the foreign weapons of war adopted by the Chinese from Western nations within the last few decades, as these do not fall within the scope of the title of this sketch. The best thing for China and the whole world would be for her, instead of following her present policy of increasing her military and naval armaments, to beat her swords into plowshares and her spears into pruninghooks, and send back all the others, duty-free, to the countries whence they came. Then shall "nation not lift up sword against nation, neither shall they learn war any more" (*Isaiah*, ii. 4).

"Weapons, however highly ornamented, are instruments of destruction. The wise man will have nothing to do with them."—MENCIUS.

The illustrations to this paper are from the *Chin t'ang shih êrh ch'ou* 金湯十二籌, *Chi Hsiao hsin shu* 紀效新書, *T'ien kung k'ai wu* 天工開物 and *Kuan shêng ti chün shêng chi t'u chih ch'üan chi* 關聖帝君聖蹟圖誌全集.

"*To Beat Swords into Plows.*—With the closing down of the Tsinan and Kaifeng Arsenals by Government order, the Arsenal Administration of the Ministry of War is planning to convert them into productive organs. The Tsinan Arsenal is to be turned into a mill for the extraction of cotton seeds oil and the Kaifeng Arsenal into a nitrate Works."—*Chinese Economic Bulletin*, April 11, 1931.

錘鐵

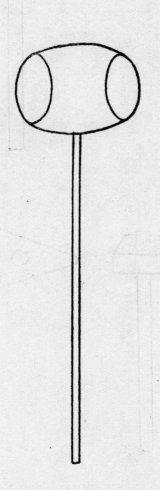

"IRON HAMMER" CLUB

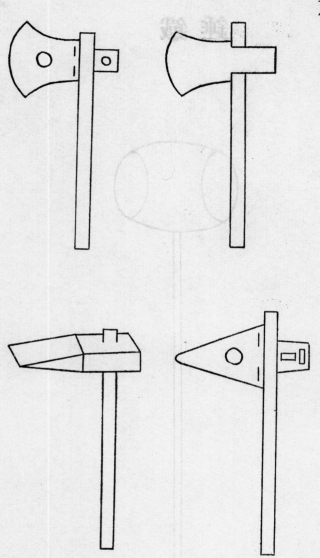

AXES
HANDLE THROUGH BLADE AND
BLADE THROUGH HANDLE

2

斧

斧鉞

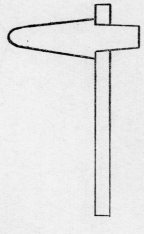

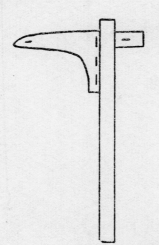

AXES

3

劔飛　　刀飛　　鎗飛

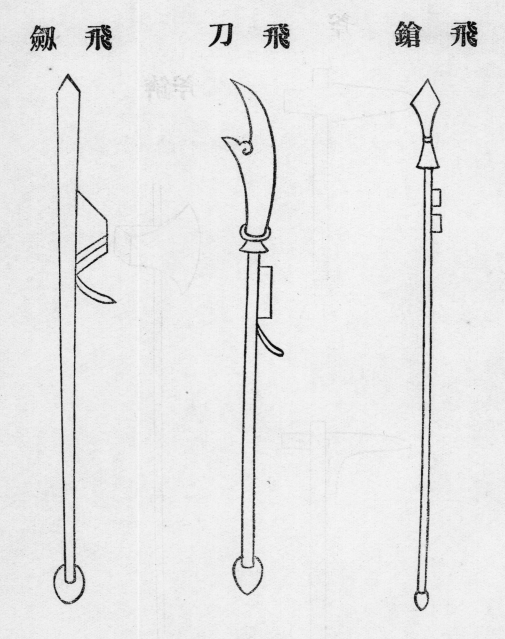

SPEARS

4

長鎗

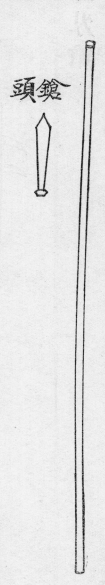

鎗頭

長鎗

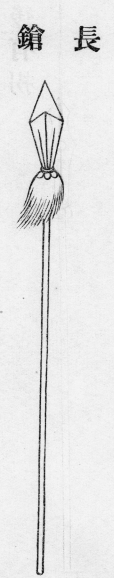

SPEARS

5

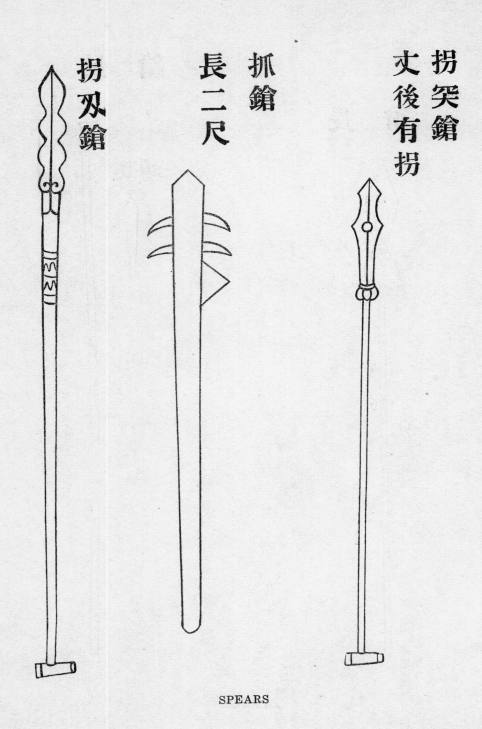

拐雙鎗

抓鎗
長二尺

拐突鎗
丈後有拐

SPEARS

6

鎗眼三　　　　　鎗鈎

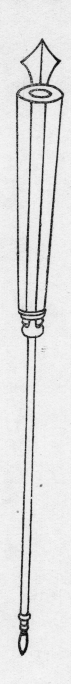

SPEARS

7

狼筅

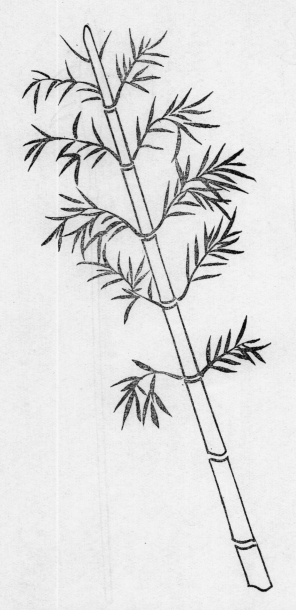

SPEAR: BAMBOO SHAFT, IRON PRONGS AND STEEL POINT

腰刀

長刀

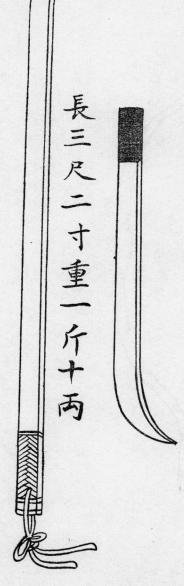

長三尺二寸重一斤十両

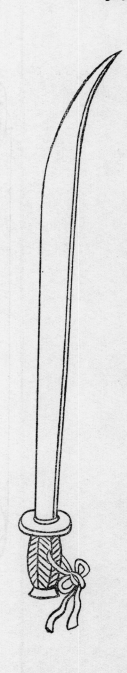

SWORDS

9

式　弓

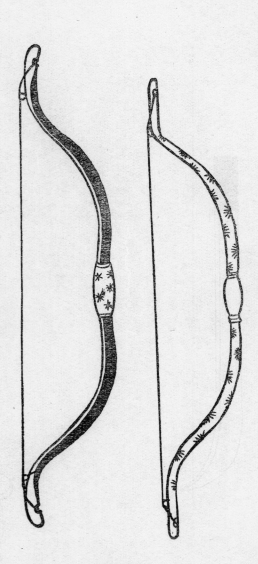

BOWS

10

弩 木

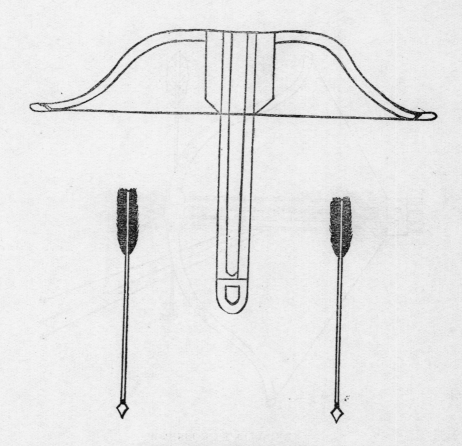

CROSSBOW AND ARROWS

箭　鬼

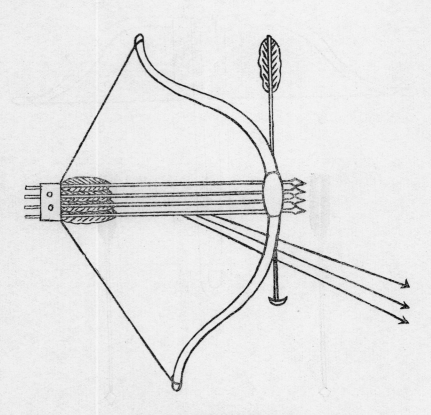

REPEATING CROSSBOW

弩 伏 河 隔

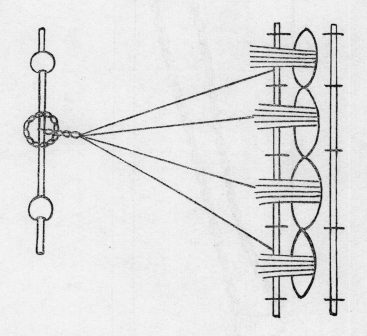

REPEATING CROSSBOW FOR SHOOTING ACROSS RIVER

石 飄

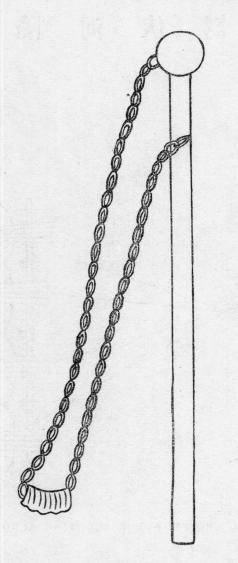

SLING

14

車　吊

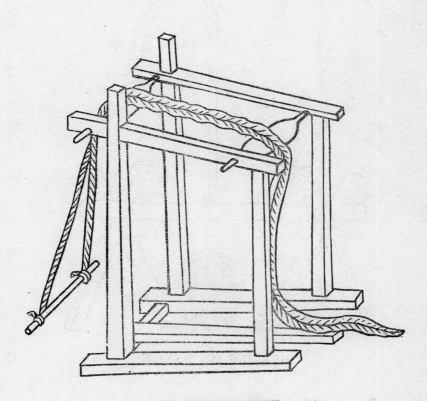

HURLING MACHINE

15

形去打起扯人用石礮

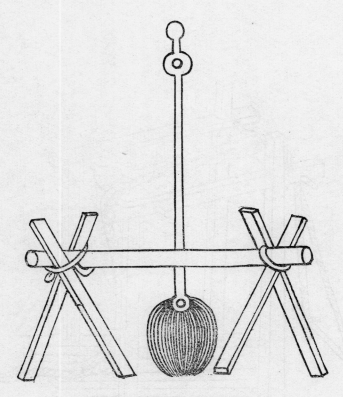

HURLING MECHANISM

架　砲

STAND FOR HURLER

17

車 砲

WHEELED HURLING-MACHINE
WITH ROPES FOR SEVERAL OPERATORS

18

車　橦

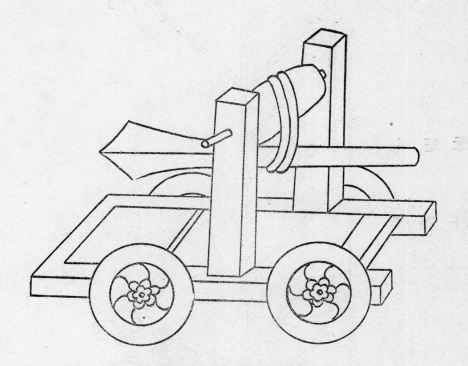

BATTERING-RAM ON WHEELED CHASSIS

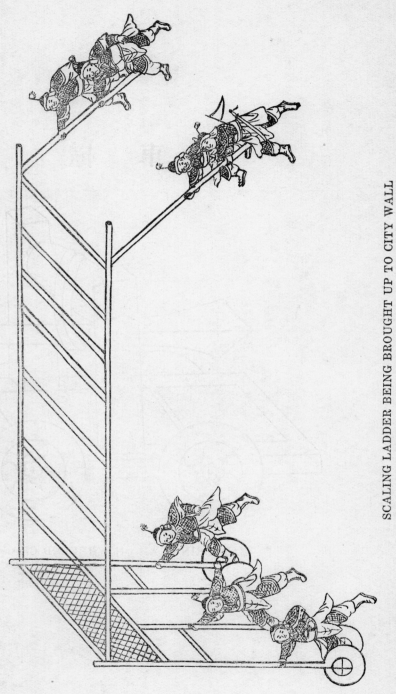

此翻梯踏雲

車未至城者

SCALING LADDER BEING BROUGHT UP TO CITY WALL

20

此翻
梯踏
車

雲車
已至
城者

SCALING LADDER AT CITY WALL

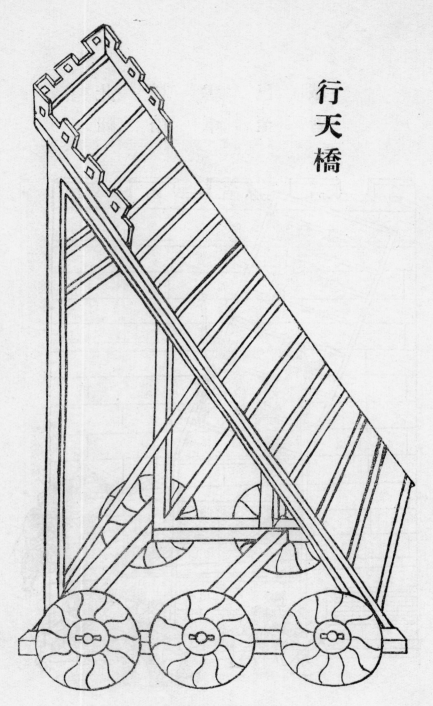

行天橋

SCALING LADDER

22

此呂公車攻城之具

SCALING TOWER WITH ARMED ASSAILANTS

23

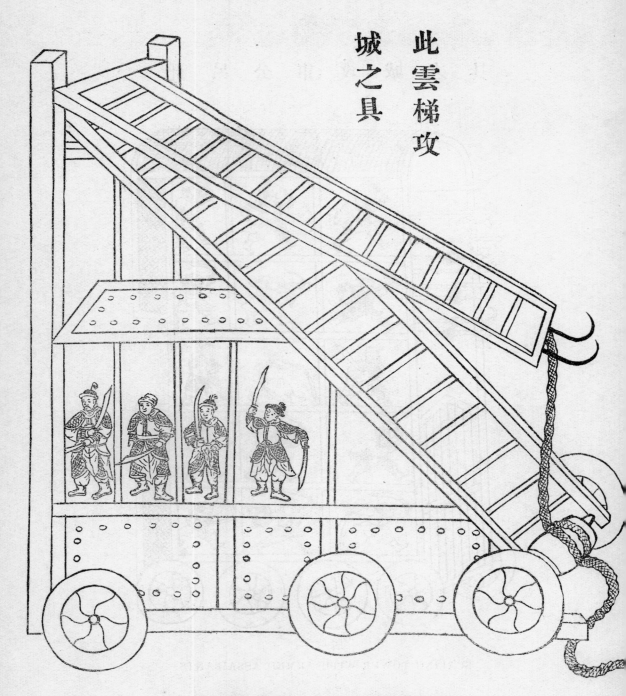

此雲梯攻城之具

ANOTHER TYPE OF SCALING LADDER

式　樓　望

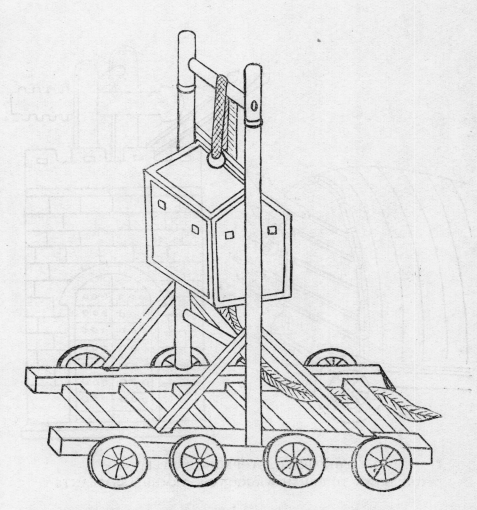

METHOD OF RAISING ATTACKERS ON TO CITY WALL

降魔杵

THE "DEVIL STOPPING PESTLE,"
CAST DOWN TO CRUSH WAGGON OF ARMED ASSAILANTS

式 牌 樣

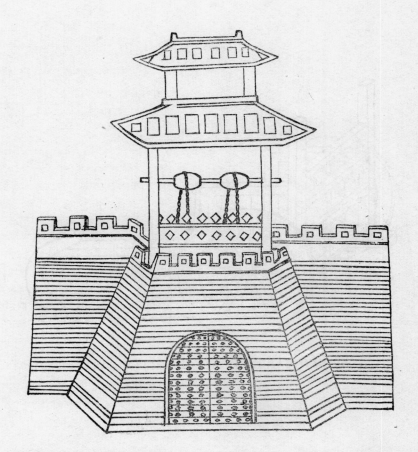

METHOD OF PROTECTING CITY GATE IF OUTER DEFENCES
ARE BROKEN IN

式 車 刀

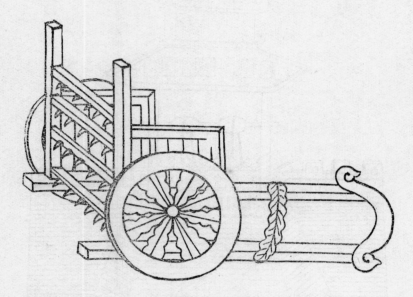

SPIKED CARRIAGE TO STOP CITY GATE

奈 何 木

奈 何 木 繫 石 蒧

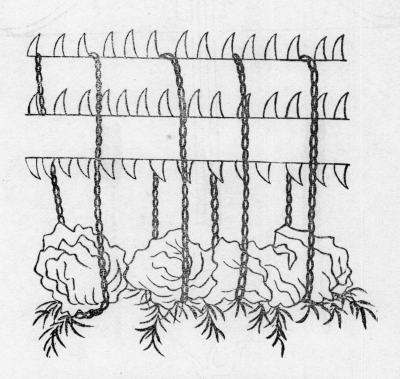

SLUNG STONES AND SPIKED BEAMS
TO PREVENT ENEMY SCALING WALL

跳鐙弩

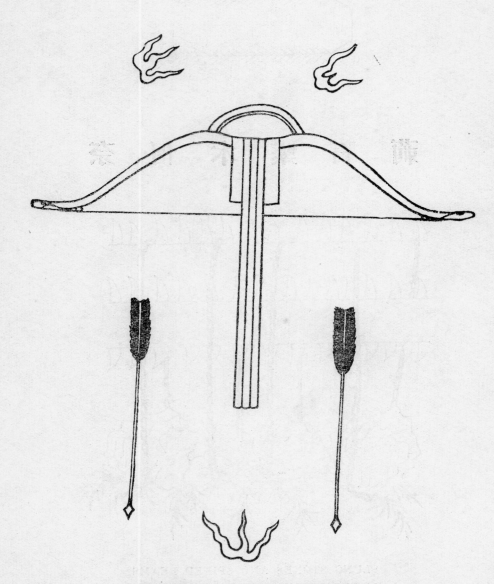

INCENDIARY ARROWS WITH BOW

30

火籠箭式

FIRE ARCHERY

31

此亦起脊對焰星

妙在此

妙在此

FO-LANG CANNON

佛狼機圖

二尺二寸三尺五寸四尺

五尺不等重亦隨之降殺

鐵門隨母銃大小子銃隨

母銃大小鐵錘隨母銃大

小火繩長二丈五尺重四

兩

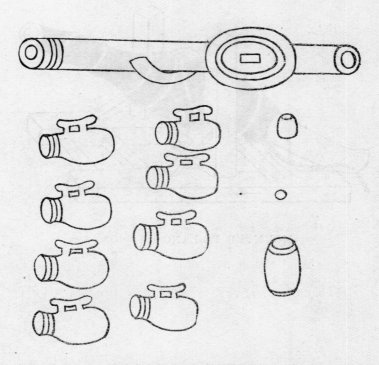

PARTS AND MEASUREMENTS OF FO-LANG CANNON

33

架佛狼機之式

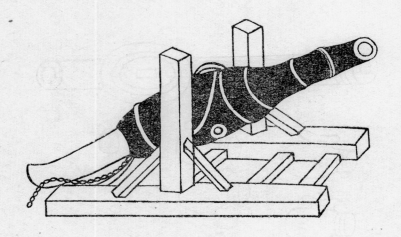

MOUNTED FO-LANG CANNON

毒龍噴火神筒式

"POISON-DRAGON" FIRE-BELCHING TUBE

35

満天噴筒式

FIRE BELCHER

式損發竹敵追鋒衝

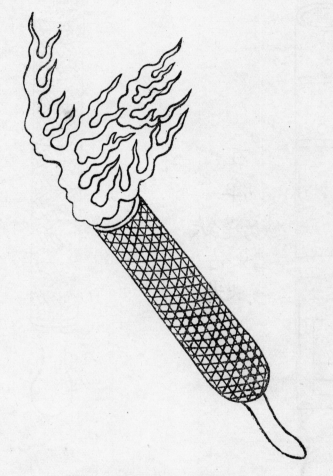

HAND GRENADE

形彈藥裝　軍將竹

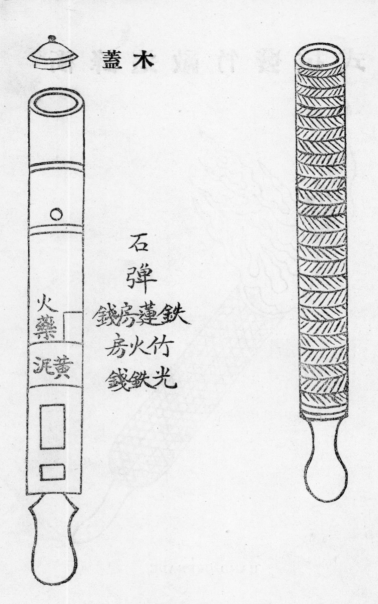

木蓋

石
彈

鉄蓮房錢
竹火房
光鉄錢

火藥
黃泥

"THE BAMBOO GENERAL"
LOADED WITH POWDER, CLAY AND
STONE BULLETS, AND IGNITED WITH TOUCH-PAPER

形分軍將

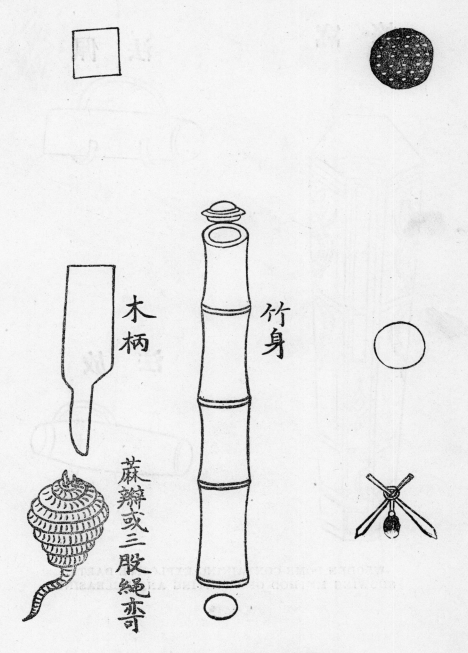

木柄 竹身

蔴辮或三股繩亦可

PARTS OF "THE BAMBOO GENERAL"

蜂窩　　佩法

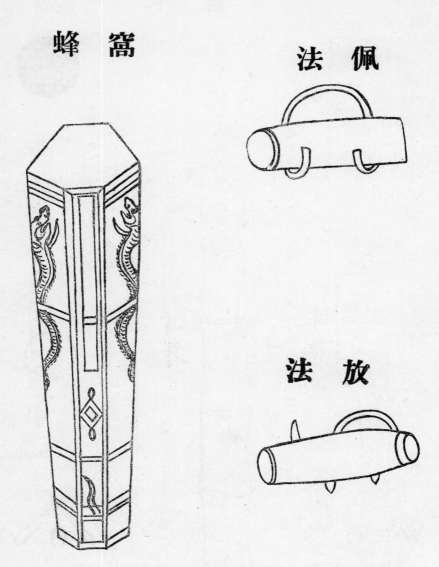

放法

WOODEN BOMB CONTAINING EXPLOSIVE DARTS.
SHOWING METHOD OF CARRYING AND RELEASING

40

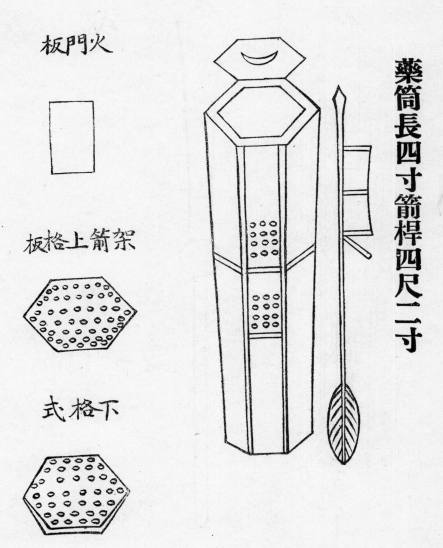

盖木　　分形

板門火

板格上箭架

式格下

藥筒長四寸箭桿四尺二寸

ROCKET WITH CASE

箭頭式

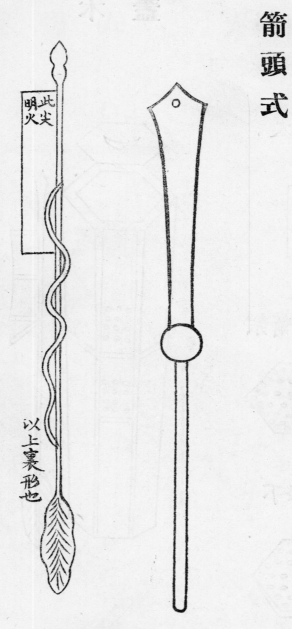

此尖明火

以上裹形也

INCENDIARY SPEAR

42

式毬火　　式燈懸

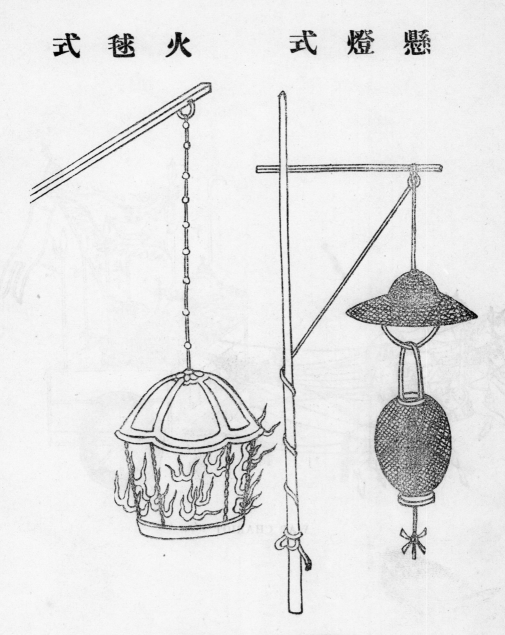

FIRE BALL AND LANTERN

WAR CHARIOT

式車神汁鉄

FIRE-SPURTER

神飛火輪舟式

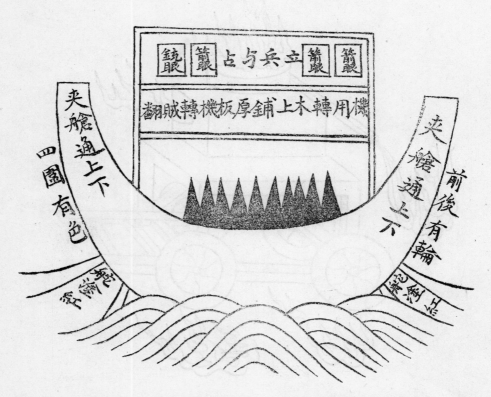

SPIKED WAR VESSEL WITH SCREEN FOR ARCHERS

沙船

SHALLOW "SAND BOAT" CONVEYING FULL COMPLEMENT
OF ARMED WARRIORS

拖 馬

HORSE SHACKLERS

48

藤牌

盾牌

SHIELDS

49

布幔

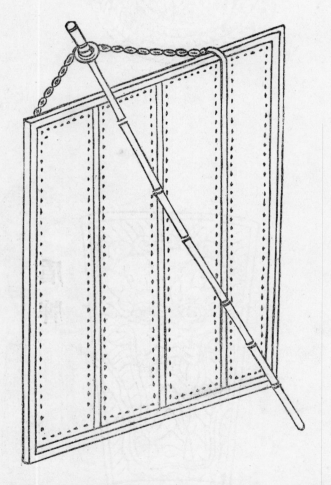

SCREEN OF THICK CLOTH FOR STOPPING ARROWS
SHOT ON TO CITY WALLS

像軍將周

COMPLETE SUIT OF ARMOUR (WORN BY CHOU GENERAL)

亢金龍

BANNER CHARM

52

丁巳神將

BANNER CHARM

53

狗郡得将

WEAPONS IN ACTION

54

大戰徐晃

WEAPONS IN ACTION
55

ANCIENT AXE-HEAD. SHANG DYNASTY

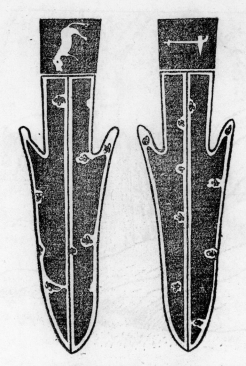

CH'Ü 戚, AXE, ENGRAVED WITH HORSE
AND BATTLE-AXE. SHANG TIME

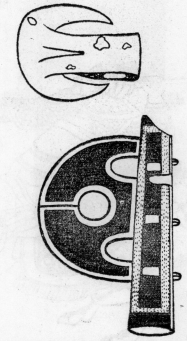

A YÜEH 鉞, STRAIGHT
AXE-HEAD. CHOU TIME

CURVED AXE-HEAD (CH'I 戚)
WITH SOCKET. CHOU TIME

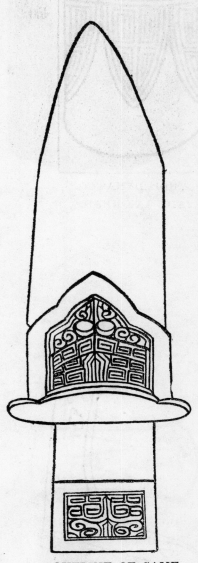

GREEN JADE DAGGER. CHOU TIME   OUTLINE OF SAME.
                                 SHOWING ORNAMENTATION

CHOU DYNASTY
JADE AXE-HEAD.

JADE AXE-HEAD. CHOU DYNASTY

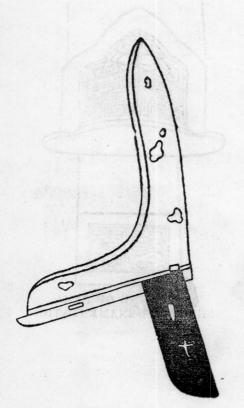

A KO 戈, HALBERD. SHANG TIME

A KO 戈, HALBERD. HAN TIME

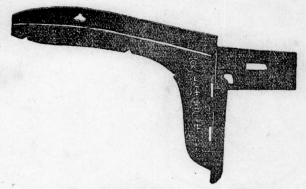

A KO 戈, HALBERD.   CHOU TIME

BRONZE SWORD.
CHOU TIME

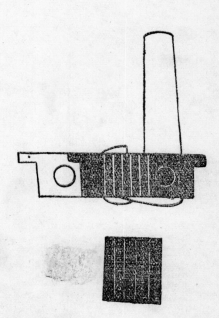

A NU CHI, BRONZE TRIGGER
OF CROSS BOW. A.D. 161